Illustrated
Book of
Mythology

Deepak MR is a professional writer and trainer with 25+ years of experience in academics, consulting, and training. He is an avid bibliophile and has studied the epics.

He is the author of the books *Abhimanyu – the warrior prince*, *Mahabharata Tales*, *Markandeya Ramayana*, *Original Vyasa Mahabharata*, *The Life and Music of Lata Mangeshkar*, *Blood & Iron*, and *Fall of the Patriarch*, and contributing author to the anthologies *Unsung Valour* and *Aryaa*.

He is currently working on a book about lessons from the Mahabharata for the modern world.

He lives in Bangalore with his wife, daughter, and parents.

Illustrated Book of Mythology
Curses and Boons

Deepak MR

Published by
Rupa Publications India Pvt. Ltd 2025
7/16, Ansari Road, Daryaganj
New Delhi 110002

Sales centres:
Bengaluru Chennai
Hyderabad Jaipur Kathmandu
Kolkata Mumbai Prayagraj

Copyright © Deepak M R 2025

All rights reserved.

No part of this publication may be reproduced, transmitted,
or stored in a retrieval system, in any form or by any means,
electronic, mechanical, photocopying, recording or otherwise,
without the prior permission of the publisher.

P-ISBN: 978-93-6156-699-8
E-ISBN: 978-93-6156-608-0

First impression 2025

10 9 8 7 6 5 4 3 2 1

The moral right of the author has been asserted.

Printed in India

This book is sold subject to the condition that it shall not, by way
of trade or otherwise, be lent, resold, hired out, or otherwise circulated,
without the publisher's prior consent, in any form of binding or
cover other than that in which it is published.

Contents

Preface ix

THE CURSE
1. Jaya and Vijaya Are Cursed 3
2. The Curse of Aged Parents 7
3. The Yakshini Cursed to be a Demoness 12
4. The Cursed Lady 17
5. Viradha's Curse and the Redemption 21
6. The Curse of Sleep 24
7. The Curse That Protected Sita 28
8. Curses That Sealed Ravana's Fate 31
9. How Matanga's Curse Saved Sugriva 35
10. Why Did Hanuman Not Know About His Powers? 38
11. The Curse That Created an Epic 41
12. Trishanku's Curse and the Legend of Vishwamitra 47
13. Yayati—The Accursed and the Curser 52
14. The Curse and the Snake Sacrifice 58
15. Yama Cursed 64
16. The Story of the Vasus, Shantanu, and Ganga 68
17. The Curse That Changed History 73
18. The Curse That Led to Duryodhana's Death 76
19. The Son Who Saved the Father Who Cursed Him 79

20. How Did Bheema Redeem Kubera's Curse?	83
21. The Curse That Made a King Turn into a Serpent	87
22. The Curses That Doomed Karna	93
23. The Curse That Made Shikhandi a Man	99
24. The Curse That Made Chandra Wax and Wane	105
25. Gandhari Curses Krishna	109
26. Two Curses for Womankind	113
27. Nachiketa Is Cursed and then gets Boons from Yama	118
28. The Curse of Parvati and the Birth of Skanda	123
29. The Curse That Led to Arjuna's Death	127
30. The Cursed Mongoose and the Sacrifice	131
31. Samba's Curse and the End of the Yadavas	136
32. How Arjuna Failed Because of Ashtavakra's Curse	141

THE BOON

33. Ravana's Boon	149
34. The Boon of Birth	152
35. The Boon That Led to the Exile	156
36. The Boon of Mighty Weapons	162
37. The Boon That Unseated a King	166
38. The Boon That Purified Souls	171
39. The Boon That Made Hanuman Almighty	176
40. The Pushpaka Vimana	181

41. Indra's Boon to Rama	185
42. The Story of the Mighty Kartavirya	188
43. How Matsyagandha Became Gandhakali	193
44. Bheeshma Gets a Boon	197
45. Vyasa's Boon and the Birth of the Kauravas	202
46. The Consequences of Kunti's Boon	206
47. Draupadi Gets Five Husbands	213
48. The Boon That Pardoned Hundred Offences	217
49. Dhritarashtra Offers Boons to Draupadi	224
50. Akshaya Patra—the Vessel of Plenty	228
51. Arjuna Gets the Celestial Weapons	233
52. How Jayadratha's Boons Failed to Help Him	239
53. How Savitri Got the Better of Yama	244
54. Indra Converts a Curse into a Boon	252
55. How Yama's Boon Helped the Pandavas in Exile	257
56. Vyasa Brings Back the Dead	263

Preface

Did you know that the first epic, the Adi Kavya Ramayana, would not have been possible without a curse? Yes, it was a curse that inspired Valmiki to write the epic story of Rama and Sita.

Vyasa, the author of the Mahabharata, became accomplished thanks to a boon his mother sought from the sage Parashara. This boon ensured he could compile the four Vedas along with the Mahabharata, which is referred to as the fifth Veda.

Curses and boons and their transformative power have played a pivotal role in our epics. The Ramayana and the Mahabharata are replete with instances where curses and boons have dramatically altered the course of events.

If Dasharatha had not been cursed, he would never have been separated from his son Rama.

If Kunti did not have the divine boon, the Pandavas would never have been born.

There are many such interesting instances from the Ramayana and Mahabharata. In this book, you can read about various curses and boons from the two great epics.

The stories of the curses and boons will immerse you in the lives of the characters from the two legendary epics. Every incident in these epics, shaped by curses and boons, has a purpose and holds lessons that are relevant even today.

Every curse was given for a reason. Similarly, every boon had a cause and effect. The story of the Ramayana and the Mahabharata is what it is, thanks to these curses and boons.

There are 32 curses and 24 boons from both the epics presented in this novel in 56 chapters containing interesting tales from our *Puranas*.

The details of each curse/boon are presented as an engaging story that helps you know what the curse/boon is, the context, the people involved, and the consequences.

At the end of each chapter, you will find a brief annotation with supplementary insights. This includes a reference to the Kanda/Parva from the Ramayana/Mahabharata, where this curse/boon can be found. The author's note provides additional details and the significance of the event, enriching your understanding.

While composing these sacred narratives, I have ensured there are no major deviations from the original source material. I have taken a few creative liberties to enhance the presentation of the story. But, I have taken sufficient care to avoid distortion of the core story in any way.

This book could not have come to fruition without the invaluable assistance of author and literary agent Suhail Mathur of The Book Bakers Literary Agency. My sincere thanks to him. I am grateful to Rupa Publications for publishing this book.

My sincere thanks to Rupa's editor Rudra Narayan Sharma and his team for the crisp editing done. Thanks again to Suhail for getting the illustrations arranged.

I would also like to thank my family members for their support while writing this book.

I would like to express my sincere thanks to fellow Indic writers and scholars - Abhinav Agarwal, Saiswaroopa Iyer, Pranshu Saxena, Bharathi V, Gaurav Tiwari, and Ratul Chakraborty, who provide valuable insights on the epics.

I hope you find as much joy in reading these *sacred stories* as I did in writing them. This book will help you get a comprehensive overview of both epics through the narration of *curses and boons*.

Deepak M R
Bangalore
www.deepakmr.com

THE CURSE

In ancient (*Puranic*) times, people were scared of being cursed. The curse was a wish expressed by someone who intended to punish another or cause negative consequences. The common belief was that the person cursing had special or divine powers that allowed him or her to deliver the curse.

It is most common to hear of sages cursing someone who has committed a sin or made a mistake. Curses could even be given by ordinary people who could invoke all their goodness and righteousness to deliver the curse.

Shapa is the Sanskrit word for a curse. The word comes from the root *Shap*, which means "to cry out loud". A curse can be a cry of anguish or anger against someone who causes the anguish or anger.

Curses can lead to different results. A celestial being can be born as a human or animal because of the curse. The curse can create a terrible situation that can lead to a person's destruction.

There are many curses mentioned in both epics—Mahabharata and Ramayana. Since the Mahabharata is a larger epic, it has more instances of curses. Many of the stories around these curses involve minor characters.

In this book, we look mainly at some of the major and significant curses that played a significant role in the two epics.

Curses could be revoked or altered by the person invoking the curse or by a higher authority or a celestial being.

There were remedies for curses. These remedies helped to reduce the impact of the curses. Many instances of such remedial measures can be seen in the two epics.

Let us explore some of the tales surrounding the invocation of curses mentioned in the Ramayana and the Mahabharata. The curses are presented in chronological order (of occurrence), with curses in the Ramayana listed first.

1
Jaya and Vijaya Are Cursed

The Kumaras marched steadily towards their destination. Sanatkumara, Sanatana, Sanaka, and Sanandana, the sons of Brahma, were on their way to Vaikuntha, the abode of Lord Vishnu, the preserver of the universe.

As they walked towards the gates of Vaikuntha, they saw the two gatekeepers, Jaya and Vijaya, standing at the entrance to regulate entry to the Lord's abode.

Jaya said, 'Brother Vijaya, look, mere children are approaching Vaikuntha. How can we allow them to disturb the Lord?'

'I agree,' said Vijaya, and he blocked the way of the four Kumaras as they attempted to pass through the gate of Vaikuntha.

'Let us in,' cried the four brothers in unison.

'We don't allow children inside,' smiled Jaya.

'The Lord is resting. Go back,' said Vijaya sternly.

'We are sons of Brahma, learned in scriptures. Let us in,' said Sanaka.

Jaya and Vijaya shook their heads, refusing to allow the Kumaras inside.

'Who are you to stop us from entering Vaikuntha?' asked an angry Sanatkumara.

'The Lord is not meant for a few people to see. He belongs to the entire world that he created. You cannot restrict us from seeing the Lord. How can you restrict children from seeing their father?' asked Sanandana.

'Do not waste our time. We will not allow you inside,' said Jaya loudly.

'You have tested our patience enough,' said Sanatana. 'Let us pass, or face the consequences.'

'Don't try to threaten us. We know what we are doing,' shouted Vijaya.

'Very well, then suffer the consequences of your mistake.'

With these words, Sanaka poured water from his *kamandalu* into his right palm. Cupping the holy water, he chanted a prayer.

His brothers followed suit.

'For stopping us, we curse you to be born on earth as mortals,' said Sanatana, pouring water on Jaya and Vijaya.

Both Jaya and Vijaya were shaken. They saw their divine weapons vanish. The curse had come into effect.

'Lord, save us,' cried the two brothers.

A blazing light appeared as though the sun itself had descended before them. Lord Vishnu had arrived! Seeing Him, Jaya and Vijaya fell at His feet.

The four Kumaras bowed to Lord Vishnu, and He blessed them.

'Save us, Lord,' cried Jaya and Vijaya.

'The Kumaras' power comes from their austerities. I cannot dispel their curse but can modify it.'

'We will accept any punishment but are not ready to leave your abode,' pleaded the two brothers.

'I place before you two options. The first one is to be born seven times on earth as my devotees. You must complete seven lives on Earth before you can return here. The second option is to be born only thrice.'

'We accept the second option,' said both brothers in unison.

Lord Vishnu smiled at them. 'You did not allow me to complete. The three times you are born, it will be as *Danavas* and my enemies. Each of these times, I will come to earth and slay you. You will be responsible for spreading evil on earth along with your fellow Asuras. I will then rid the earth of this evil by vanquishing you and your cohorts. This will fulfil a third of your curse. Once you are slain the third time, you will return here, free from the curse's effects.'

The two brothers bowed to the Lord, accepting the modified curse. He smiled at them as they vanished from Vaikuntha.

■

The above story is not actually a part of the two epics. It comes from the *Bhagavata Purana*. It is an important story and the curse within it is significant as it impacts the two epics.

In the *Satya Yuga*, Jaya and Vijaya were born as the Rakshasa brothers Hiranyaksha and Hiranyakashipu. Vishnu, as Varaha, killed Hiranyaksha.

When Hiranyakashipu harassed his own son Prahlada, a devotee of the Lord, Vishnu incarnated as Narasimha, the man-lion Avatar, and killed Hiranyakashipu.

In *Treta Yuga*, they became Ravana and Kumbhakarna, slain by Vishnu as Rama. In *Dvapara Yuga*, they were born as Dantavakra and Shishupala, slain by Krishna.

After three mortal lives as Vishnu's enemies, Jaya and Vijaya returned to Vaikuntha, freed from their curse.

2

The Curse of Aged Parents

The young prince Dasharatha, destined to rule Ayodhya, was in his prime, enjoying life and honing his archery skills.

After an evening of hunting, the prince was returning to his kingdom. His expert charioteer raced away, as usual, taking him far ahead of his guards and friends. He was a little distance away from reaching his kingdom when he passed by a *sarovara* (lake).

Hearing a sound, Dasharatha asked the charioteer to stop.

'I hear an animal drinking water,' Dasharatha whispered. 'It must be big, perhaps an elephant. Let me finish my hunt with one more kill.'

'My Lord,' whispered the charioteer. 'It is so dark, and it is not possible to see anything. How will you hunt the elephant'?

Fixing an arrow to his bow, Dasharatha listened carefully to the sound. Closing his eyes, he turned around in the direction of the sound. Pulling back the arrow to his shoulder, the prince released the arrow, and it went racing through the air.

Smiling, he said, 'With the skill of *Shabdavedhi*, I can hit any target by sound.'

The arrow found its mark, and there came the sound of something breaking, followed by a scream.

Dasharatha's heart leapt. It was not the sound of an animal scream but that of a human.

Shocked, Dasharatha ran to the riverbank and froze at the sight before him.

Illuminated by partial moonlight, a young man lay dying, blood oozing out of his chest. Dasharatha's arrow had found its mark.

Running to the young man, Dasharatha pulled out the arrow. Blood came gushing out of the wound as the prince tried desperately to stop the bleeding.

He cradled the young man's head on his lap and shed tears, for he had reduced a young man in the prime of his life to this situation.

Gasping for breath, the young man pointed to the distance. Dasharatha could see a fire burning in front of a temple.

'My parents need water,' gasped the young man before dying on Dasharatha's lap.

Dasharatha understood what had happened. The young man was filling the pot with water for his parents. Hearing the gurgling sound made by water entering the pot, Dasharatha had mistaken it for an animal. He had committed the unforgivable act of killing a helpless young man.

Dasharatha took out a vessel from his chariot with a heavy heart. He filled it with water and trudged towards the temple in the distance.

As he came near the temple, he heard the voice of an old man. 'Son Shravana, have you brought the water?'

'No, dear husband,' said the voice of an old woman. 'That is not the sound of my son's footsteps. It is someone else.'

The blind old couple turned towards Dasharatha.

'I have brought you water,' he said.

'I don't want water from you, my child,' said the old man. 'I am Shantanu, and this is my wife, Malaya. Our beloved son Shravana Kumara is taking us throughout Aryavarta so we can visit various holy lands before our lives end.'

Touching a stick with two baskets at each end, the old man said. 'Our son loves us so much that he carries us in the baskets and takes us everywhere. Truly, we are blessed to have such a son.'

'Did he come with you?' asked Shravana's mother eagerly.

Dasharatha could not hold back his emotions any longer.

'NO' he said in a choking voice, trying to hold back his tears. 'I have brought water for you. Please drink it.'

The old man got up with a jerk and moved towards Dasharatha. He moved his hands around, trying to touch the prince. He felt the prince's face and then, bringing his hands down, held Dasharatha by the arm.

'Where is my son? I fear the worst. Tell me what happened to him.'

'Forgive me. I am a prince, and I was hunting. Accidentally, I killed your son. He told me before dying to give you water. Please drink this water first.'

The old couple collapsed on the ground, wailing inconsolably even as Dasharatha tried to help them get up.

They pushed him away and bemoaned their fate for losing their young son.

'Take us to our son,' ordered Shantanu.

With a heavy heart, Dasharatha held the old couple by their arms and took them to their son's body.

Falling on the ground, they touched their son's body and wept uncontrollably.

After some time, Shantanu said, 'O prince, it is good that

you told the truth. If not, your head would have shattered into a hundred pieces. We do not want water from you. Help us cremate our son.'

Shedding tears, Dasharatha helped the old man cremate his son and perform his last rites by the river.

Turning to Dasharatha, Shantanu said, 'Because of your arrogance, we lost our only son, who lived to care for us. You have burdened us with his cremation.'

'I am sorry. Let me care for you as my parents.'

Malaya laughed, 'Young man, there is no one in the world like my son. You have extinguished not just one life but three lives. We do not wish to live in a world without our son.'

Shantanu held his wife's hand. Turning to the prince of Ayodhya, he said, 'O Prince, we are suffering from grief at having lost our beloved son. I curse you, prince! One day, may you also suffer in the same way as we are suffering. You will die separated from your son, unable to see him for the last time before you give up your life.'

Uttering this curse, the old man clasped his wife's hand and dragging her with him, entered the fire that burnt his son's body.

Even as the flames raged, reducing the three bodies to ashes, Dasharatha collapsed on the ground, bemoaning how one mistake had destroyed an entire family.

Years later, Shantanu's curse came true. Dasharatha sent his son Rama into exile and died in agony, unable to see him again.

■

This story, part of the Ayodhya Kanda, is a poignant reminder of how one reckless act can destroy lives.

3

The Yakshini Cursed to be a Demoness

Tataka and her sons Subahu and Maricha ran towards the sage Agastya's ashrama, screaming in rage.

'He killed my husband. I won't spare him,' yelled Tataka, brandishing an axe in her hand. Her sons let out bloodcurdling roars, holding assorted weapons in their hands.

Agastya sat in front of the sacrificial fire quietly without flinching, watching the three Yakshas charge at him.

When she reached near, he raised his hand, stopping her in her tracks.

'Your husband was drunk, and he created a nuisance in the hermitage. Even though he was warned, he tried to defile our rituals. I had no option but to kill him. So, go back to where you came from.'

Yelling in uncontrollable rage, Tataka continued to charge towards the sage.

He picked up his kamandalu and took some water. Uttering a chant, he flung the water at Tataka, uttering these words, 'I curse you and your vile sons to become corpse-eating demons. You will lose your beautiful form and will become an ugly monster.'

No sooner did Agastya utter these words Tataka and her sons turned into grotesque creatures. Losing their human-like appearance, they grew horns and had tusk-like teeth protruding from their drooling mouths. Seeing her body change, Tataka wailed in shock. She ran from there crying loudly, followed by her sons.

Tataka then stayed in a forest with her sons, becoming a corpse eater and competing with wild animals for food. Eventually, she began preying on humans. She became a terror, slaughtering people in and around the forests. She and her sons would venture out, attacking ashramas and disturbing rituals performed by sages.

People started avoiding the forest where she lived, fearing for their lives. News of her terror spread far and wide. The news reached the sage Vishwamitra, who then took the princes of Ayodhya to the forest.

As they entered the forest, they were greeted by the sounds of chirping birds, which made a raucous sound, warning everyone in the forest that there were intruders. As they moved through the forest, there was a deathly silence. No animals were to be seen as they moved to the centre of the forest.

They soon reached a clearing where a dilapidated temple stood. Surrounding the old building were piles of skeletons with bones scattered about. The stench of rotten flesh was all-pervading.

Sitting in front of the old building was a monstrous female. It was the dreaded Tataka.

'Rama,' said Vishwamitra, addressing the heir of the kingdom of Ayodhya. 'This is the reason I brought you here. Kill her and rid this forest of her evil presence. Let the people of this place breathe easily. Let rituals go on unabated without her vile intrusions. Kill her now, Rama.'

'Respected guru,' said Rama. 'She is a woman. How can I kill her? Isn't it a sin to kill women?'

'Rama, it is your *dharma* to get rid of evil. It doesn't matter whether the evil comes in the form of a male or female. Vishnu killed the wife of the sage Bhrigu when it was needed. Go ahead and do your duty. There will be no sin attached to this killing.'

Seeing the three of them, Tataka roared in fury. She got up, towering over the trees. Displaying her foot-long sharp nails, she charged towards them.

Rama and Lakshmana fixed arrows to their giant bows and, having drawn back the strings released them. The arrows raced through the air and struck Tataka on her chest. Roaring with pain, she pulled out the arrows, broke them, and threw them away.

Looking around for a weapon, she uprooted a tree and flung it at the princes of Ayodhya. Shooting a volley of arrows, they smashed the tree into pieces.

She then picked up a huge rock, crushed it into tiny bits in her palms, and flung the pieces, creating a rock shower. Lakshmana fixed five arrows in his bow and shot the arrows. Even before the arrows had left the bow, he fixed five more arrows and released them. Soon, a shower of arrows smashed each of the stones hurled at them.

Rama fixed a golden arrow to his bow and, aiming, released it. The arrow blazed through the air and struck Tataka in her heart. Moaning in pain, the demoness clutched her chest. Desperately trying to regain her balance, she failed and fell to the ground, causing the earth to shake.

The demoness Tataka was dead, and Rama had rid the world of an evil scourge.

Tataka was a Yakshini who was cursed to be a demoness. Ram slew her and ended the terror she had unleashed on innocent people and sages. A beautiful Yakshini, her life was ruined thanks to her mindless decision to attack a great sage. The sage's curse led to her death at the hands of Vishnu's incarnation.

This story is from the *Bala Kanda* of the Ramayana. Vishwamitra comes to the court of King Dasharatha and, with his permission, takes Rama along with Lakshmana to help him eradicate the world of demons and other evil beings. Tataka is among the first of the demons to be killed by Rama.

4
The Cursed Lady

Gautama was furious. The sage shook with rage, his nostrils flared, and his eyes red.

Taking a deep breath to regain control, Gautama spoke in a trembling voice, 'You cheated on me. How could this happen?'

'Forgive me, husband. I was deceived,' said Ahalya, weeping.

'You cheated on me with Indra! How can I accept this?' shouted Gautama.

'Listen to me, husband,' she said. Indra came disguised as you. I thought it was you showing me love after so long. I didn't know it was him.'

'You lie!' thundered Gautama. 'Are you not a *pativrata*? Can you not tell the difference between me and someone disguised as me? You are unworthy of being my wife.'

'Believe me. I was deceived. Wouldn't have gone to Indra in his own form.'

'But you gave yourself to him when he came looking like me? So will you give yourself to every man disguised like me?'

'That's very unfair,' said Ahalya, looking up at her husband. 'It is your fault for not giving me the love I desired. When Indra approached me, I was ecstatic that my husband was showing love for me after such a long time. Indra is cunning and knows everything, so he took advantage of the situation.'

'You are a sinner, Ahalya. You have committed a sin for which there is no repentance. I will never forgive you for betraying me. I have never even looked at any other woman, whereas you have given yourself to another man and enjoyed the experience.'

'I am the victim, not the sinner,' cried Ahalya, her eyes glowering in anger. 'Indra is the sinner, not me.'

'Indra will not escape my curse. His lust will cost him his manhood. As for you, your betrayal as a *pativrata* is greater. I curse you to remain here alone for thousands of years, invisible, without sustenance, and unseen by anyone.'

No sooner did Gautama utter the curse than Ahalya faded away. She was shocked to see her limbs slowly disappear. She was becoming invisible.

'Please, husband, do not punish me so harshly. Is there no redemption?'

Gautama turned to walk away from the ashrama. As he walked away, he said, 'You will suffer for hundreds of years, after which the Lord Vishnu will come here. That is when you will be redeemed from your curse.'

Even as Ahalya turned invisible and became a part of the dust in the ashrama, Gautama left the place and went to the Himalayas.

Hundreds of years later, the sage Vishwamitra came there. The princes Rama and Lakshmana, the sons of King Dasharatha of Ayodhya, were with him.

Vishwamitra narrated the story of Ahalya and told Rama. 'O Rama. I brought you here because it is ordained that you should come here. When your feet touch the dust in this hermitage, it will touch Ahalya, who is a part of the dust. The touch of your feet will purify and redeem her from her curse.'

Hearing his teacher's words, Rama stepped into the hermitage. When Rama's feet touched the ground, the dust rose and formed a cloud. From it emerged Ahalya, redeemed from her curse.

Ahalya worshipped Rama, who blessed her as celestial flowers showered from the sky.

Hearing footsteps, Ahalya looked up. It was her husband, Gautama. He bowed before Rama and then embraced his wife.

'You are redeemed from my curse. Thanks to the blessings of Rama of Ayodhya, you are now pure again. I happily accept you again as my wife.'

After sending off Rama, Lakshmana, and Vishwamitra, the reunited couple lived happily in the hermitage.

■

Ahalya's tale, from the Bala Kanda of the Ramayana, highlights her redemption after being cursed for Indra's deceit. Indra's sin caused him to lose his manhood, later restored by the Gods.

The popular story about Ahalya depicts her as having been turned to stone. The story narrates how Rama's foot touched the stone, causing the curse to be redeemed. But the Valmiki Ramayana tells this story differently. The *Bala Kanda*, in which this episode is narrated, says that Ahalya was cursed to be invisible and recumbent in the dust.

Gautama's curse and Ahalya's eventual redemption bear deep parallels to Sita's own trials. While Ahalya erred and faced punishment, Sita—despite her unwavering virtue—was subjected to relentless scrutiny and forced to prove her purity. Yet, when the world continued to question her chastity, she chose not just to escape humiliation, but to reclaim her dignity by returning to the Earth, her divine mother, rather than endure the agony of endless doubt.

5

Viradha's Curse and the Redemption

Rama, Sita, and Lakshmana walked through the Dandakaranya forest, enjoying its beauty and vibrant life.

Suddenly, a mighty demon charged toward them, smashing through the trees.

The huge demon stood before them and growled, seeing the three of them. The demon grabbed Sita and strode away, smashing trees in his path.

Rama and Lakshmana froze in shock. The demon stopped in his tracks. Turning towards the two brothers, he said, 'You two dress like sages but wield weapons. You must be bandits. You are unworthy of a beautiful woman like this one. She will be my wife from now on.'

With these words, the demon turned to go away.

Rama, overwhelmed by the sight, said to his brother, 'Losing my kingdom and father was painful, but this is unbearable. How can I let anyone touch Sita?'

A furious Lakshmana assured his brother, 'I will not forgive this demon. I will kill him and bring back Devi Sita to you.'

Viradha stopped after hearing these words. Turning back, he asked, 'Who are the two of you? Where are you going? Why did you step into this forest?'

Rama declared loudly, 'We are Kshatriyas from the

kingdom of Ayodhya. Who are you to stop us from moving in this forest?'

The demon announced, 'I am Viradha, with a boon from Lord Brahma that no weapon can kill me. So, go away before I drink your blood.'

Rama's response was to fix seven arrows to his bow. Taking aim, he released the seven arrows in an instant. The arrows streaked through the air and struck the demon, causing him to shriek in pain.

Putting down Sita, Viradha charged with a spear, but Rama and Lakshmana destroyed it with arrows. Roaring, the demon swatted their arrows and grabbed them.

Lakshmana glanced at Rama, anticipation flickering in his eyes, awaiting his brother's next move.

Rama said, 'Let him take us where he wants. Let us

see where he takes us. Right now, Sita is safe, and that's all that matters.'

Viradha took the two brothers deep into the forest. Seeing the demon take away her husband and brother-in-law, Sita cried, 'Stop, leave my Rama. Let the brothers go free, demon. Take me instead.'

Hearing Sita's voice, Rama struck the demon on the face, and Lakshmana followed suit. The two brothers pummelled Viradha until he released them from his vice-like grip.

They unleashed a barrage of arrows, severing Viradha's arms and legs, causing him to collapse.

They repeatedly struck him with arrows and hit him with their fists, but the demon refused to die. That is when Rama decided they would bury him alive.

He asked Lakshmana to dig a bottomless pit to bury the demon.

That's when Viradha stopped resisting and addressed Rama. 'Rama, your blows helped me remember my past. I was a Gandharva cursed by Kubera to live as a demon until Vishnu, in human form, freed me.'

Hearing these words, Lakshmana dug a bottomless pit, and the two brothers pushed Viradha into it. They then closed the pit, burying him alive. Before returning to Sita, they placed stones around the place to create a burial ground.

Rama once again united with Sita, and the three continued on their journeys through the forest.

∎

This story from the *Aranya Kanda* of the Ramayana reflects the recurring theme of Rama redeeming curses, foreshadowing Sita's future abduction.

6

The Curse of Sleep

Chaos reigned as beings of all kinds ran in panic, their cries drowned by a ferocious roar.

It was not a pride of lions causing the noise but a rakshasa. A rakshasa was devouring up all that he saw. He grabbed people, animals, and all living beings and chomped on them, ripping them apart and swallowing them.

This was possible thanks to his monstrous size. He was twice the height of a tree, with a mouth as vast as a palace gate. The gigantic demon with the gargantuan appetite was Kumbhakarna, the son of the sage Vishravasa.

The sage Vishravasa's union with a rakshasi resulted in three sons, including Kumbhakarna, known for his monstrous appetite.

The third son was a monstrous being, Kumbhakarna, named so because his ear resembled a pot.

By a quirk of nature, he grew at an unbelievable rate, rapidly increasing in age and size. Soon, he was a giant with an appetite bigger than his size. When he was hungry, he went berserk. He would eat anything that walked, flew, or moved. His preference for the flesh of humans and celestials made him a terror.

Soon, the scene of the monstrous feasting on flesh and blood became a daily feature. The panicky celestials ran to their King Indra and told him what was happening.

Indra, enraged, set out to confront Kumbhakarna mounted on his majestic elephant Airavata.

'Stop,' said Indra. 'Desist from this barbaric act; else you will face my wrath.'

Kumbhakarna looked at Indra and flung a half-eaten carcass at him.

Indra hurled his Vajra, striking Kumbhakarna with thunderous force. The thunderbolt found its mark, striking Kumbhakarna in the chest, and he tottered.

The assembled celestials cheered their King. Alas, their celebrations were short-lived. Balancing himself, Kumbhakarna wiped the blood from his chest. Roaring in rage, he leapt in the air at Indra. Grabbing Airavata's tusk, he broke it, pulling one half out.

He jumped on top of Airavata, standing on the great elephant's head. Holding the broken tusk of Airavata, he plunged it into Indra's chest like a knife. The tusk tore into Indra's chest, causing blood to gush out.

Crying out in pain, Indra held on to his elephant tightly to stop himself from falling. Kumbhakarna laughed at Indra. Holding the elephant by its trunk, he flung it away. Indra and his elephant went spinning in the air back to their abode.

A chastened Indra went to meet Brahma and complained about everything that was happening. Brahma decided to see what was happening.

Even Brahma was momentarily alarmed by Kumbhakarna's ravenous assault.

Regaining his composure, Brahma poured water from his *kamandalu* onto his palm. Chanting a powerful hymn, he threw the water at Kumbhakarna, uttering a curse, 'Your father Vishravasa seems to have created you to eat up the entire world. If I don't stop you, you will eat up the entire world's inhabitants. I curse you to sleep forever.'

The moment the water fell on Kumbhakarna, he collapsed to the ground, losing consciousness. Soon, he was snoring.

Ravana came running to the creator and pleaded with him, 'O Brahma deva, my father Vishravasa is your son, and so Kumbhakarna is your grandson. Is eternal sleep the punishment you give to your grandson? Show mercy, my Lord.'

Brahma thought for a while and told Ravana. 'He will sleep for six months and then wake up for one day, after which he will continue to sleep. If you wake him up early, his life will be in danger.'

With these words, Brahma disappeared. Ravana stood silently, watching his colossal brother sleeping. His only thought was how to carry his brother back to his palace.

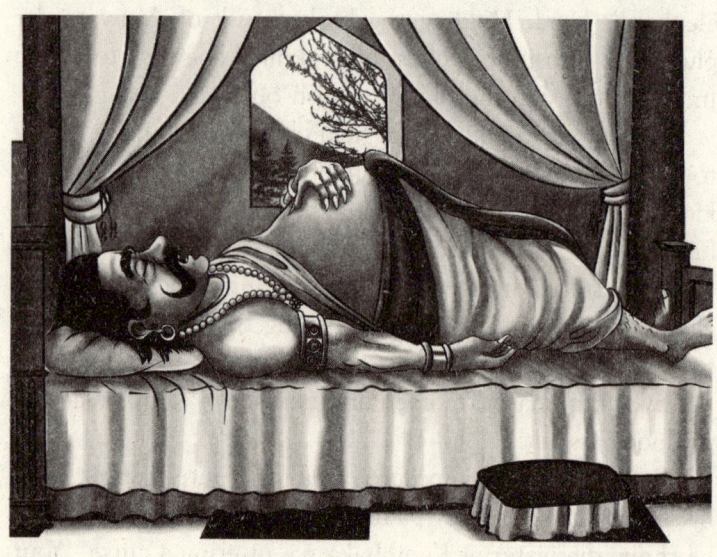

The popular story of Kumbhakarna sleeping is that he wanted to ask for a boon, but Goddess Sarasvati sat on his tongue and made him ask for *Nidratvam* (sleep) instead of *Nirdevatvam* (destruction of Gods).

But the *Yuddha Kanda* of the Ramayana has Ravana explaining that Kumbhakarna's curse is because of a curse from Lord Brahma. Unable to defeat Rama, Ravana wakes up his brother forcibly before the six months are over. Kumbhakarna battles Rama and is killed.

Interestingly, the *Uttarakanda* of the Ramayana has the popular version of the failed boon instead of the curse. The difference between these two chapters of the Ramayana is a reason some people believe the *Uttarakanda* is not a work of Valmiki and was written by someone else later.

7
The Curse That Protected Sita

Brahma was meditating in silence when Punjikasthala, Varuna's daughter, rushed in, weeping for justice. Falling at Brahma's feet, she pleaded for justice. Brahma gently asked her to explain her plight.

Opening his eyes, Brahma looked at the sobbing nymph.

'Get up, child. Tell me, why do you cry?'

'I want justice, O Father of the world. The vicious Ravana has violated me.'

'Tell me what happened?' asked the creator.

While flying, Ravana intercepted me in the Pushpaka Vimana and expressed his vile intentions.

'What happened then?'

I fled, but Ravana captured and violated me before discarding me cruelly.

Brahma, enraged, declared Ravana a sinner and vowed to prevent such acts in the future.

With a gesture, Brahma summoned Ravana, who bowed before him and noticed Punjikasthala.

Brahma glared at Ravana, and his gaze was so fierce that Ravana was forced to bend down before the creator of the world.

'I curse you, Ravana. You will not molest any woman henceforth. If you dare to violate any woman in the future without her permission, your head will split into a hundred pieces.'

Brahma then waved his hand in dismissal, and Ravana disappeared.

Brahma's curse saved womankind, including Sita, from Ravana.

■

The *Yuddha Kanda* mentions this curse, which Ravana himself later recounts as the reason he could not harm Sita. He expressed his inability to touch Sita without her consent because of Brahma's curse.

The curse of Brahma thus saved Sita from a terrible fate. While some myths portray Ravana as wise, his deeds reveal a vile nature; an act of *adharma*. He had violated many women in the past, which is why he was cursed.

When he tried to molest Vedavathi, she immolated herself. Vedavathi was then reborn as Sita. There is also a reference to Ravana molesting the *apsara* Rambha. Ravana's actions burdened the earth, leading Vishnu to incarnate as Rama to vanquish him.

Both the Ramayana and Mahabharata feature incidents of a woman being humiliated. All the people who carried out this vile act in both the epics met with a gruesome end. The epics convey a very significant lesson that all those disrespecting women will be destroyed.

8
Curses That Sealed Ravana's Fate

Ravana flew proudly in the Pushpaka Vimana, a unique vehicle he had taken from his brother Kubera after conquering Lanka.

The Pushpaka Vimana could fly anywhere, and Ravana loved to explore the world in his vehicle. This time, he was moving to the northern mountainous regions of the Himalayas. He watched the vast mountains from above the clouds and marvelled at the snow and ice.

Soon, he came across an enormous mountain with ice

on it. He moved the vimana up in the air, but the mountain towered over him. He kept moving the vehicle up but still found the mountain blocking his way. The mountain's summit seemed unattainable.

Furious at the mountain blocking his path, Ravana tried and failed to find a way around it.

Thoroughly frustrated, he moved the vehicle down, trying to find another route. At the bottom of the mountain, he saw a being with the head of a bull, who smiled mockingly at him.

A furious Ravana shouted at the being, 'Who are you? How dare you mock me?'

'I am Nandi, and I was laughing at seeing your antics trying to cross this mountain. This is Kailasa, the abode of the Lord of the three worlds, the God of Gods. None can cross the mountain without his permission.'

'Ha,' said Ravana. 'Are you a man, yaksha, celestial, animal, or a mutant? You are a creature without a proper face, and you dare mock me, the one with ten heads?'

'The number of heads does not matter, only what's inside them,' mocked Nandi.

'You dare insult me? With a head like that and the way you jump around, you are just a monkey. Talking to monkeys like you who live in the mountains is below my dignity. Get lost from here.'

Nandi, angered, retorted, 'You insult me and my master. You'll regret this.

'I care neither for you nor your master, stupid monkey,' snorted Ravana.

You mock monkeys, but one day they will be your downfall,' cursed Nandi.

Ravana laughed loudly. 'I neither fear you nor the

monkeys you predict will destroy me. I have a boon from Brahma that makes me virtually immortal. I will show you my power. I will pick up this mountain and throw it aside so I can move ahead.'

With these words, Ravana descended to the base of the mountain. Descending from his Vimana, he let out a deafening roar, his ten heads and twenty arms expanding in fury. With a tremendous yell that shook the earth, he pressed against the mountain's base, wedged his hundred fingers beneath, and began to lift it.

Nandi was flabbergasted to see Ravana lift Kailasa.

On the top of the mountain, Parvati lost her balance as the mountain shook. Disturbed by the shaking mountain, Shiva opened his eyes.

'Mahadeva, someone is making the mountain shake. Who can it be who dares to do such a thing?'

Shiva smiled. 'It's Ravana, arrogant enough to lift Kailasa.

Enraged, Parvati cursed Ravana to be killed by Vishnu's incarnation.

Shiva moved slightly. Bringing down his foot, he struck the mountain hard with his toe. The mountain came down hard, and its entire weight fell on Ravana's fingers. He screamed in pain, tears running down his eyes. He realised he had made a big mistake. Try as he could, he was unable to move the mountain.

Realising his mistake, Ravana praised Shiva until he was forgiven and returned to Lanka.

■

The story of Ravana being cursed by Nandi and Uma is mentioned in the *Yuddha Kanda* of Ramayana. Ravana, after suffering losses in the battle with Rama, realises his mistakes. He admits he made a mistake not asking Lord Brahma to make him invincible to humans.

He recollects the curse of Parvati and Nandi that led to this situation. The curse of Nandi had already come true, as the mighty monkey Hanuman had come to Lanka, burnt the city, causing him severe humiliation.

As per the curse of Parvati, he died at the hands of a man. The man was none other than Rama, the prince of Ayodhya, who was the incarnation of Vishnu.

9
How Matanga's Curse Saved Sugriva

Rama sat listening to Sugriva's tale, with Lakshmana at his feet and Hanuman by Sugriva's side.

'I understand your problem. You have promised to help me find my wife, Sita. You are now my friend, and it is my duty to help you. I will help you defeat your evil brother Vali, who drove you out of your home and took your family hostage.'

Sugriva bowed to Rama. 'Thank you, prince of Ayodhya. I love my brother but must kill him to reunite with my family.'

Sugriva explained how he mistook Vali's fight with the demon Mayavi for his brother's death and sealed the cave entrance.

'Why did you not wait for your brother for some more time?'

'I did wait, O noble Lakshmana. I waited for a year outside the cave. When no one came out, I blocked the cave entrance after seeing the blood. How was I to know my brother had survived and it was the demon that died? My brother was not ready to listen to my explanations. It hurt when he accused me of trapping him in the cave for the sake of the kingdom.'

'You should have explained the situation,' suggested Lakshmana.

My brother's temper forced me to flee to this mountain, where I found safety.

'How is this place, Rishyamukha, safe for you? Why didn't Vali follow you here to kill you?'

'This is the mountain where the sage Matanga lives. Many years back, Mayavi's father, Dundubhi, challenged Vali to a fight. Dundubhi had taken the form of a buffalo. The two fought for a long time, but Vali got the better of Dundubhi and killed him. Holding the demon by its horns, he threw him high in the air, and he landed here.'

'What happened then?'

'Dundubhi's carcass defiled sage Matanga's yajna, leading to a curse that prevents Vali from stepping onto this mountain.'

Rama assured Sugriva, 'Challenge Vali. I will help you

defeat him and reunite with your family.

A happy Sugriva looked at the faithful Hanuman and smiled in anticipation of defeating his brother and reuniting with his family.

∎

The story of Vali and Sugriva is narrated in the *Kishkinda Kanda* of the Ramayana. This is yet another story from the Ramayana that refers to a curse. The sage Matanga cursed Vali and this curse helped save Sugriva's life. It also put him in the right place to meet Rama, who was travelling in that area searching for Sita.

Rama then killed Vali, and Sugriva became the king of the *Vanaras*. Later, he helped Rama by sending a band of his monkeys to find Sita.

10

Why Did Hanuman Not Know About His Powers?

The monkeys looked on worriedly at the vast ocean in front of them. It was the largest water body they had ever seen. They could not see the land of Lanka that lay beyond the ocean, and they worried about how to cross it.

Angada, the nephew of the Vanara king Sugriva, was leading a band of monkeys in search of Sita. Sugriva sent groups of monkeys to find Sita, and Angada's team learned from Sampati that she was in Lanka.

They knew they had to cross the ocean, and that it was impossible to swim across. The Vanaras were well-known for their ability to jump long distances. But it was clear that they could not jump as far as Lanka.

Jambavan, the eldest and wisest in the group, addressed Angada.

'O Angada, we cannot return empty-handed, especially after knowing that Mother Sita is in Lanka. We have to cross this ocean, and the only way to do this is to take a mighty leap.'

'Who can jump so far? Maybe I should make the attempt. It is better than returning after failing in the mission,' said Angada sadly.

'Who?' asked all the monkeys in unison.

'Hanuman,' said Jambavan, pointing to the mighty monkey seated quietly on a rock.

'Can I really jump so far? I have never tried it,' said Hanuman.

'There is nothing you cannot do. You do not know your own powers. You have forgotten all that happened in the past. It is the right time to remind you.'

Jambavan then reminded Hanuman of his childhood. You were born to Anjana and Vayu, the wind god.

'As a child, you mistook the Sun for a ball and caused havoc, leading to boons from Brahma that you would be the mightiest being on earth and a *chiranjeevi* who would not know death.'

'But then why do I not know about my powers?' asked Hanuman.

'The sages cursed you to forget your powers until the time came to use them for a noble cause.'

'It's time to use your powers, Hanuman. Grow in size and leap across the ocean to find Sita.'

With Rama's name on his lips, Hanuman grew tall and leapt across the ocean.

Invoking his regained powers, Hanuman became tall and huge. With the cry 'Jai Shree Ram' on his lips, he leapt across the ocean and proceeded towards Lanka to find Mother Sita so they could reunite her with Rama.

■

In the *Kishkinda Kanda*, Hanuman regained his powers, marking the beginning of Ravana's downfall.

An interesting fact is that Hanuman's mother was none other than Punjikasthala, who had been violated by Ravana. She avenged her insult by giving birth to the mighty Hanuman, who was responsible for the destruction of Ravana's forces.

11

The Curse That Created an Epic

Valmiki was walking down the bank of the river Ganga. He stood and bowed to the sun, peeping out from behind the mountains in the distance. He entered the river to complete his morning oblations.

As Valmiki left the river, he noticed a pair of herons on a nearby tree, engrossed in their mating ritual.

Fascinated, Valmiki marvelled at nature's cycle of life and creation.

With his eyes fixed on the birds, Valmiki's mind marvelled at the cycle of life, death, and creation. He had a beatific smile, feeling joyful at the pleasant sight of creation happening before his eyes.

It was an enjoyable way to start the day. A sudden whooshing sound broke Valmiki's reverie.

An arrow had raced through the air and struck the male bird. The bird struggled in pain for a few seconds before falling to the ground and dying. The female screeched in shock, agony, and bewilderment, not able to understand what happened to her mate.

Valmiki then saw a Nishada tribal hunter running towards the tree. He bent down and picked up the dead bird, retrieving his arrow. Seeing the female bird jumping up and down beside its dead mate, the hunter reached out to catch the bird.

That's when Valmiki lost his temper. The act of creation that was going on so peacefully was brutally disturbed by cruel death. This was no way for the poor bird to die, especially while it was still mating with its partner.

'You vile hunter!' screamed Valmiki.

Startled by Valmiki's voice, the hunter turned, dropping the dead bird.

He saw an elderly man whose clothes were wet with water, having finished his morning ablutions. The man seemed to be pious and looked like a sage. His eyes were glowering, and the intensity in his eyes sent a chill down the hunter's spine.

'O hunter, you have killed a pair of herons engaged in the act of mating. For this sin, you are eternally doomed never to achieve a state of rest.'

The hunter was stunned to hear the curse. He stammered, trying to justify his deed, but could not look at the eyes of the fearsome hermit in the lake. Bending his head low, the hunter quietly walked away from the place with dejection writ on his face.

Valmiki stood silently, tears streaming as he watched the mourning female.

After a long time, the female realised that her dead partner would not come back. Crows had gathered, ready to feast on the dead bird. The female bird flew away, never to come back to the riverbank again.

With a deep sigh, Valmiki got out of the lake, saying a prayer for the poor dead bird whose carcass was now being ripped apart by crows.

Valmiki suddenly realised that the curse he uttered was special. The way the words were spoken and the arrangement of words and syllables were unique. Valmiki could not believe that he was capable of such a speech.

As he prepared to return, he recalled what had happened the previous day. He had been sitting with his disciples deep in prayer when he realised that he had a visitor. It was none other than the celestial sage Narada.

Valmiki was astonished to see his visitor. He had never expected to receive a visit from such a noble personage.

Narada visited Valmiki and narrated the story of Rama, the slayer of Ravana.

He concluded by saying, 'Whoever reads the story of Rama will be blessed. His sins will be liberated, and he will achieve all he desires.'

Standing by the riverbank, he understood the true meaning of all that happened. Narada had indirectly asked him to write the story of Rama. But could he? He hardly knew how to compose a sentence. How could he write the great story in such a way that reading it would release a person from his sins?

The meaning of the curse he uttered was now clear. The curse revealed the structure for composing Rama's story.

He turned to his disciple, Bharadwaja, who had accompanied him, and said, 'The quatrain I uttered was special. The position of the letters makes it suitable to be sung as a song while it conveys a clear message. This verse came out of my grief or *shoka*, hence I will call it *shloka*.'

When Valmiki returned to his home, he had another guest. Brahma appeared uninvited, honouring Valmiki with his presence.

After being worshipped by Valmiki, Brahma said, 'You now know the story of Rama. You also know how to write this story. So complete this onerous task and compose the Ramayana–the ballad of Rama. This legend will exist and be read as long as rivers and mountains are on this earth.'

Having conveyed this advice, Brahma disappeared.

Valmiki then set out to compose the Ramayana.

■

The story of Valmiki and his cursing the heron is a part of the *Bala Kanda* of the Ramayana. It is the introductory part that explains how the Ramayana was written. It was a divine blessing that made Valmiki curse a hunter in a particular way. This led to the creation of the concept of a *shloka*, which henceforth was used to write poems.

The *Ramayana*, the first kavya or epic poem (*Adi Kavya*), was written by Valmiki. As Brahma prophesied, the *Ramayana* will endure as long as the world exists. Even today, its legacy continues through books, stage performances, television shows, and films, cementing Valmiki and his work as integral to our history.

While the *Ramayana* portrays Valmiki as a holy man who shelters Sita, raises Lava and Kusha, and reunites them with Rama, it does not delve into his backstory. A popular legend suggests that Valmiki was initially a thief. When asked by a man if his family would share in the sins he committed while stealing, Valmiki discovered that they refused. Distraught, he wandered aimlessly until seven sages advised him to chant "Rama." Struggling to say the name, he began chanting "Ma-ra," which eventually became "Rama."

Another version claims Valmiki was originally a Brahmana named Agni Sharma, later renamed after performing intense austerities that caused an anthill (*Valmika*) to grow around him. Some believe he was a Brahmana called Lohajangha, who turned to theft to survive during a drought. There is also a belief that Valmiki was reborn as Tulsidas, the author of the *Ramacharitamanas*.

Regardless of his origins, Valmiki is celebrated as the *Adi Kavi*, or the first poet, of India. Prayer sessions today, where chapters of the Ramayana are read, stand as tributes to the great man who immortalised the story of Ramachandra of Ayodhya.

12

Trishanku's Curse and the Legend of Vishwamitra

Once King Trishanku, of the Ikshavaku dynasty met the great sage Vasishta.

'O great sage, I desire to enter Heaven in my physical body. I have a plan to achieve this goal and seek your support.'

Vasishta replied, 'O King, none can enter Heaven in their own body unless blessed by the Gods. I cannot help you in achieving this impossible task.'

Trishanku did not give up hope. He decided to approach the sons of Vasishta, who were well-versed in rituals.

'After the great Vasishta, I respect you the most. I want you to perform a ritual to help me reach Heaven in my physical form. Your father did not help me, but I request your help.'

'You disregard Sage Vasishta's words. We cannot help you,' declared the sons of Vasishta.

'Very well,' said Trishanku. 'If you don't help me, I will seek someone else to fulfil my wish.'

This enraged the sons of Vasishta. They cursed Trishanku, saying, 'Your behaviour does not befit that of a king. You deserve to be a *Chandala*. We curse you to be a *chandala* who takes care of the dead in cemeteries.'

Cursed, Trishanku became a chandala, stripped of his former life. Bereft of his kingdom, Trishanku decided to approach the great sage Vishwamitra.

Bowing his hands before Vishwamitra, Trishanku said, 'O great sage, the sons of Vasishta have cursed me to be a chandala. All I wanted was a ritual to help me ascend to Heaven, and now I have been cursed to this fate.'

Vishwamitra then told Trishanku, 'I, Vishwamitra, will do what Vasishta and his sons could not. I will help you by performing rituals that will help you reach Heaven. This is my promise to you.'

Vishwamitra began the ritual with powerful chants.

The ritual commenced with the sages chanting hymns and offering ghee to the sacrificial fire. As the ritual reached completion, Vishwamitra prepared the oblations for the Gods. Acceptance of the offering would lift Trishanku's curse.

But the Gods never came to receive the oblations. Vishwamitra was infuriated that the Gods refused to grace his sacrifice.

'Listen, Trishanku. If the Gods deny you Heaven, I shall send you there with my own power. I hereby command you to rise to Heaven. Rise Trishanku and ascend to Heaven.'

Even as Vishwamitra uttered these words and lifted his right hand, Trishanku began to float in the air, moving towards the Heavens. The assembled sages and others looked on in astonishment.

Just as Trishanku was about to enter Heaven, Indra stopped him. 'A cursed chandala has no place in Heaven. Return!'

Indra then pushed Trishanku, making him fall back to earth. Trishanku screamed in horror as he fell head-first from the skies. Seeing him fall, Vishwamitra raised his hands and said, 'Stay! Stay!'

This stopped Trishanku's fall. An angry Vishwamitra said, 'I shall create a Heaven and stars for you, proving my power.'

Hearing this, the Gods were upset. They immediately appeared before Vishwamitra and said, 'Do not do such a thing, O sage. We cannot allow a *chandala* cursed by Vasishta into Heaven.'

'I have promised Trishanku I will send him to Heaven, and I cannot make my words go false.'

'Then, let him remain where he is and let it be his abode and his own Heaven,' suggested the Gods.

'Very well,' said Vishwamitra. 'Trishanku will stay in this place forever. This will be his Heaven. The stars I have created will continue to stay, and Trishanku will henceforth be a star in the sky.'

The Gods decreed that Trishanku's Heaven would be where he remains.

Vishwamitra was happy with the compromise and agreed to it. Trishanku thus remained upside down in a world in between Earth and Heaven surrounded by stars. He could not enter Heaven, but the power of Vishwamitra ensured Heaven was where he was.

■

The story of Trishanku is found in the *Bala Kanda* of the Ramayana. The story is featured in the epic to highlight the power of Vishwamitra. Being a rival of Vasishta, Vishwamitra was ready to help Trishanku because Vasishta had not helped him. Though he was born a Kshatriya, Vishwamitra became a great sage. He earned powers through the merit of his penance, austerities, and rituals.

The story demonstrates how powerful the sage was. The story also teaches us about excessive greed and the results it can bring. Trishanku wanted to enter Heaven but ended up in a state of suspended animation, neither in Heaven nor on Earth. Such a situation is commonly referred to as '*Trishanku stithi* (condition)'.

It is believed that the stars Vishwamitra created formed the Centaurus constellation in the sky. It is also believed that Trishanku finally became the star Alpha-Centauri since it is midway between Earth and the next constellation (which could be interpreted as Heaven). Trishanku is a word used to denote a situation that is neither here nor there or a state of confusion.

Legends claim Vishwamitra attempted to create his own universe before compromising with the Gods.

13

Yayati – The Accursed and the Curser

Yayati, the king of Aryavarta, paced up and down in his chambers. He was now alone in his chambers. His wife had left him and gone, which was natural. What worried him was what would happen next. He knew Devayani would have gone to meet her father.

His wife's father was Shukracharya, the most learned sage, who was the preceptor of the *asuras*. When he had given his daughter to Yayati for marriage, he had extracted a promise from Yayati to keep her happy.

What happened next was not Yayati's fault. Devayani insisted that her friend Sharmishta come along with them as her maid. She was doing this spitefully to insult her friend and avenge an old incident when Sharmishta had pushed her into a well after a fight.

That incident had worked out well for Devayani because it was Yayati who had saved her from the well. It was love at first sight for the King, who was besotted by her beauty. He had then married her with the permission of her father.

Devayani insisted that Sharmishta accompany her as a maid. Sharmishta had no option but to comply because her father, the King of Asuras, depended on Shukracharya. Not complying with Devayani's words could lead to the sage leaving the land of the *Asuras*.

Devayani was taking an enormous risk by taking the beautiful Sharmishta to the place where Yayati would be in touch with her daily. Shukracharya knew the risks involved and had warned Yayati not to cheat on Devayani.

Yayati broke his promise and fathered children with Sharmishta.

Soon, he had three children by Sharmishta, in addition to the three children Devayani had given him. He tried his best to manage both his families without Devayani coming to know but failed. Devayani found out the truth, and she was wild with rage. She walked out of their home.

The Queen leaving the palace was not a good sign. But what Shukracharya would do worried him more. He knew the sage could curse him, and that made him fearful.

As he paced, pain gripped his legs, and he found himself stooping.

Reeling at his wrinkled hands, he rushed to the mirror in horror.

Yayati stood in front of the mirror and was shocked by what he saw. He saw an old man in the mirror. He could not recognise himself since his hair had turned white and his face was wrinkled.

It was Shukracharya's doing! It was clear what had happened. Devayani had complained to the sage, and he had delivered a curse, turning Yayati into an old man.

Yayati ran out, holding the wall for support. He screamed for his guards and aides. They were all stunned to see how their king had turned into an old man.

With their help, he climbed into the chariot and collapsed in the seat. The charioteer rode the chariot at a blazing speed, taking him to the ashrama of Shukracharya.

He reached the ashrama and saw the sage by the river, finishing his evening rituals. Stumbling and finding it difficult to walk on the rocky riverbank, he walked to the sage with great difficulty and fell at his feet.

'Placing the sage's feet on his head, Yayati pleaded, 'Great sage, forgive me. I have sinned and seek your mercy.'

'Rajan,' said Shukracharya. 'I knew this would happen, so I warned you. As a king, you should be in control of your senses. How can you control a great country if you cannot control your senses?'

'Forgive me, great sage. I am but a man who has desires, not a sage who has the power to hold the senses in check. I agree I deserve punishment, but not this. How can I rule this great country in this condition? My kingdom and citizens will suffer because of this curse. Please take back your curse, great sage.'

Shukracharya thought for a while and said, 'Yayati, even I cannot take back a curse once I have uttered it. However, I can change my curse. If any of your sons exchange their youth with you, then this curse can be redeemed. Ask one of your sons to become old, and you can become young again. This is the best I can do for you.'

Yayati took the blessings of the sage and left for his kingdom, helped by his aides. As he left, he saw Devayani standing by the door of the ashrama, watching him bereft of expression on her face.

On reaching his palace, Yayati summoned his sons and addressed them. 'My son, I have become like this because of Shukaracharya's curse. I have an empire to rule, and I have many desires to fulfil. I was in the prime of my life and wanted to experience life to the fullest. As my sons, it is your duty to help me. Please exchange your youth with me so I can live a youthful life again. Once I fulfil all my desires, I will return your youth.'

Devayani's eldest son Yadu bowed, and said, 'Father, I have not even started experiencing life. Without youth, what good is life? How can I give up my youth and lose everything even before I have gained it? Forgive me, I cannot help you.'

Yayati turned to Yadu's brother Turvasu, who said, 'Forgive me, father. I also have desires and a life to live. I want wives and children and want to enjoy the pleasures of life. Sorry, I cannot do this.'

Next was the turn of Sharmishta's son, Druhyu, refused, citing his right to enjoy life.

His brother Anu Anu, too, declined, unwilling to live as an old man.

Yayati was shattered hearing all his sons reject his plea. He turned to his and Sharmishta's youngest son, Puru, and pleaded, 'My dear son, you are but a young man who has experienced nothing in life. I know you will decline me, but please consider my plea. Since you are a child, you will not become too old. Allow me to enjoy life for some time and then I promise to return your youth.'

Puru fell at his father's feet and took his blessings. He said, 'I am ready, father. I will become old and lead a quiet life of renunciation. The day you give me back your youth, I will enjoy what life offers me.'

Yayati was thrilled to hear his young son's words. He hugged him and wept in joy.

Turning to his other sons, he said, 'I regret fathering all of you. What good are sons who do not help their father in need? I curse you all. None of you will inherit my kingdom, nor can you live here. Leave my kingdom and go wherever you want.'

Embracing Puru, he said, 'You are my heir. You will be the next king and such a mighty king that your successors will be known as Pauravas.'

Yayati then enjoyed youth for many years. Even as Puru remained old, Yayati fulfilled all his desires. All the pleasures available in the world—food, women, and wealth were enjoyed by him to the fullest.

Finally, Yayati summoned Puru and said, 'My son, I have indulged enough to learn that true joy lies in renunciation.'

With these words, Yayati returned his youth to Puru, who took over as the King. Yayati spent the rest of his life in the forest practising severe austerities. Soon, he gave up his earthly life and went to Heaven.

Thanks to the merit earned by his austerities, he enjoyed unrestricted access to all that Heaven offered. This offended Indra, who used the flimsy excuse of an argument to throw Yayati out of Heaven.

As Yayati fell, he encountered his grandsons, the children of his daughter Madhavi. Hearing Yayati's tale, the four grandsons offered their grandfather the merit they had earned through their good deeds.

By virtue of these merits, Yayati once again ascended to Heaven. Pleased by their sacrifice, the Gods rewarded Yayati's grandsons, Shibi, Vasumana, Ashtaka, and Prattardana, by permitting them to enter Heaven.

Yayati then lived in Heaven along with his grandsons.

■

The story of Yayati is narrated in the *Adi Parva* of the Mahabharata. The sage Vaishampayana narrates the story of the ancestors of Emperor Janmejaya. He tells the story of Yayati, the curse that made him old and how it was redeemed.

Yadu, who was thrown out by his father, established his own kingdom, and his successors were known as Yadavas (ancestors of Krishna). Turvasu moved out of the border of his father's kingdom and ruled over the Yavana kingdom (believed by some to be Greece). Druhyu formed the Twipra kingdom, while Anu formed a tribe known as the Tusharas.

Puru ruled as the Emperor of the world and was well-known for his wisdom and his might. His successors were known as the Pauravas. Later on, his successor, Kuru, became famous, after which this clan was known as the Kuru clan.

14

The Curse and the Snake Sacrifice

Sage Jaratkaru was a wandering hermit. One day, as he was climbing a mountain, he came across a cave where he saw people hanging upside down in the cave.

He entered and asked who they were.

One of them replied, 'O Jaratkaru, we are your ancestors. Because you have no son, we are suffering in this state, unable to go to Heaven. So, we are continuing our austerities hanging upside down. If you take a wife and get a son, we can attain Heaven.'

Jaratkaru told his ancestors, 'I agree, but I will only marry a woman named Jaratkaru.'

Jaratkaru then went to the forests and prayed for a wife. He then heard a sound and saw a celestial being before him. It was Vasuki, the king of the snakes.

'O Sage, I heard your prayers. I offer you the hand of my sister. Marry and live happily with her, for she too is wise and an adherent to *dharma*.'

'What is your sister's name?' asked Jaratakaru.

'Her name is the same as yours,' said Vasuki. 'She is called Jaratkaru because, just like you, her body has become lean by performing austerities.'

The sage was happy hearing this and married the snake princess. He led a happy life with her, and soon, a child was born to them. They named the child Astika. The birth of the child led to the ancestors of the sage being released from the caves and attaining Heaven.

Vasuki rejoiced at the birth of Astika, for he had long awaited this moment.

The reason for Vasuki's joy was what Brahma had told the Gods many years ago.

Kadru, the mother of the snakes, had made a bet with her sister Vinata, the mother of Garuda. She had wagered that the divine horse Ucchaishravas had a black tail, while Vinata had said the horse's tail was white.

Kadru had summoned her sons, the Nagas, and had asked them to cover the tail of Uchchaihshravas and turn it black so she could win the wager. The snakes refused. Kadru cursed her sons for disobeying her, dooming them to perish in a future snake sacrifice (Sarpa Satra).

The Gods had then approached Brahma, who told them that the son of Jaratkatu would be the one who would stop the sacrifice and prevent the destruction of the Naga race.

Parikshit, son of Abhimanyu, ruled Hastinapura. One day, the king was returning after a hunting expedition when he saw a deer and hit it with an arrow. The deer ran away into the ashrama of a sage. Parikshit followed it and saw the sage Shamika in the ashrama.

'Have you seen the deer I shot, O holy one?' asked Parikshit.

The sage remained silent, and an enraged Parikshit placed a dead snake around his neck. The sage had not replied because he was undergoing a vow of silence.

When his son Shringi learned of this, he was furious and cursed the king.

'The vile king who insulted my learned father in this

way will die by the same species he used to humiliate my father. I curse the king to die on the seventh day from today, bitten to death by none other than Takshaka, the king of snakes.'

When Shamika came to know of the curse, he was unhappy. He sent his disciple, Gourmukha, to inform the king of the curse.

The king's ministers and generals built a palace on pillars in express time, and lodged the king there. They guarded it such that no snakes could enter it. They were determined to prevent the king from being killed by Takshaka.

On the seventh day after the curse, a group of Brahmanas came to meet the king but were not allowed to do so. Nagas in disguise gifted Parikshit a basket of fruit. Parikshit looked at the basket of fruits and picked up the most succulent-looking fruit. He bit into it and saw a worm.

'My Lord, there is a worm. Throw the fruit away,' said a minister.

'Don't fear. The sun is now setting, and the seven days are over. No one can harm me now. The sage's curse has failed.'

He then laughingly placed the worm on his throat. As the sun set, the worm transformed into Takshaka.

The mighty snake raised its golden hood and bit the king on his throat. Parikshit collapsed, his body turning blue, gasping for breath. Even as the king died, Takshaka flew away from there, spewing venom everywhere. The venom caused a fire, and the entire palace burned down causing widespread panic.

After Parikshit died, his son Janmejaya became king and ruled the Hastinapura empire well. One day, the sage Uttanka arrived and criticised the king for not avenging his father's death. When Parikshit learned how a curse had led to his father's death, he blamed Takshaka for it.

'The snakes are a venomous race. They, along with Takshaka, need to be destroyed. I will organise a great snake sacrifice. In that sacrifice, the entire snake clan will be wiped out.'

Janmejaya organised the *Sarpa Satra*, drawing countless snakes into the fire.

When Takshaka clung to Indra for support, the sages uttered powerful chants that dragged Indra towards the fire. A panicky Indra fled, leaving Takshaka to fall towards the fire.

Just as Takshaka was about to fall into the fire, a voice was heard. 'Stay! Stay!' said the voice.

Janmejaya was surprised to hear the voice. It was a young ascetic who was none other than Astika, the son of Jaratkaru. Janmejaya welcomed the sage and honoured him.

'Ask anything you want, O sage. I will grant you your wish,' said Janmejaya.

'Then stop this sacrifice,' said Astika.

Astika pleaded for the sacrifice to stop and spare the Nagas.

On the advice of the assembled sages, Janmejaya stopped the sacrifice. Takshaka and the other surviving Nagas were saved. Thus, Astika had saved his clan from extermination.

■

The story of the snake sacrifice is narrated in the *Adi Parva*, at the beginning of the great epic, the Mahabharata. The epic begins with the sage Souti narrating the incidents of the *Sarpa Satra* to Shounaka and other sages in the Naimisha forests. Souti narrates the curse of Kadru. He also tells the story of Parikshit being cursed, leading to his death.

The young sage Astika played a key role in preventing the extermination of the Nagas. Many Nagas had been eliminated by Arjuna and Krishna after the burning of the Khandava forest. Takshaka had escaped at that time. He once again escaped death thanks to the son of Jaratkaru.

All the sages of that time took part in the snake sacrifice, including Vyasa. The disciple of Vyasa Vaishampayana narrated the Mahabharata to King Janmejaya during the sacrifice. Vaishampayana narrated the stories of Janmejaya's ancestors and the Great War, thus leading to the first public narration of the Mahabharata.

15

Yama Cursed

The sage Mandavya was deep in meditation. Entirely focused on his austerities, he was oblivious to all that occurred around him in his ashrama. He remained unaware as thieves hid stolen goods in his ashrama.

The thieves then hid in different places within the ashrama. Soon, the guards came in pursuit of the thieves and saw the sage. The Chief of the guards asked, 'O revered sage, did you see any robbers?'

Mandavya was so deep in meditation that he did not hear the guards. They started to search the ashrama when the sage did not reply. The guards found the stolen gems and stones. They searched around and found the hidden robbers.

'I suspect this hermit is involved with the robbers. That is why he is keeping quiet. Let us take him also to the king,' said the leader of the guards.

The guards then dragged the astonished sage with them to the palace. Tied in chains, Mandavya was made to stand along with the robbers.

The king, who was in a bad temper, did not even bother to listen to Mandavya's protestation of innocence.

'Impale them on stakes as a lesson to others.'

'O King, I am innocent,' pleaded Mandavya, but the king ignored him.

The guards took Mandavya along with the robbers and

impaled them on sharp wooden stakes. After a few hours, the robbers died a painful death, but Mandavya lay on the stake with its sharp edge protruding from his stomach. He neither died nor cried but continued to perform his austerities.

Seeing this, the Brahmanas of the city went to the king and told him he had made a mistake. The king hurried to where Mandavya was impaled and was stunned to see that the sage was not dead.

'Truly, you are a great soul, and this sharp stake will not cause your death. I have made a mistake in punishing you thus. Forgive me, great sage,' said the king, his arms folded in salutation.

The sage replied, 'It is not your fault, Rajan. It is my destiny that led me to this fate.'

The king ordered the sage to be removed from the stake. Unable to remove the stake, the guards cut it, leaving a piece inside him.

Because of the piece of stake that was lodged in his body, Mandavya came to be known as Animandavya. He was well-respected for his wisdom and the strength of his austerities.

After many years, the sage died and was brought before the God of death, Yama. 'O Yama, why did you punish me unjustly for a crime I did not commit?'

'O sage, I do not punish anyone without justification. Once, you had impaled an insect on a sharp blade of grass, causing it immense pain. The punishment you underwent was because of the sin you committed.'

O Yama, I was a child, unaware of right and wrong when I committed this act. You violated your own law.

Hearing the sage's words, Yama was left speechless.

The sage cursed Yama, 'O Yama, I curse you to be born on earth to a low-caste woman, your penance ending only after your rebirth.'

Yama bowed to the sage and accepted his curse.

Yama was then born in the palace of Hastinapura as Vidura. He was the son of Parishrami, the maid of Queen Ambika. His father was the great sage Vyasa. Vidura would grow to be a learned and wise man known for his adherence to Dharma. He became the Prime Minister of the kingdom of Hastinapura.

Vidura followed Dhritarashtra into the forest, where he merged his soul into Yudhishtira, ending Yama's curse.

■

The story of Mandavya, his curse to Yama, and the birth of Vidura are all a part of the *Adi Parva* of the Mahabharata. Vidura was born to a Shudra woman and was known as a Kshatta. He was known for his wisdom and tried many times to advise Dhritarashtra to make peace, but his advice fell on deaf ears.

Yudhishtira, the eldest of the Pandavas, was the son of Dharma or Yama. This is why Vidura, an incarnation of Dharma, merged his soul into that of the son of Dharma. Vidura's existence on earth ended, and Yama was freed from the curse of Animandavya.

16

The Story of the Vasus, Shantanu, and Ganga

While in the forest, the Vasus came across Sage Vasishta's ashrama. In that ashrama was the divine cow, Surabhi. The cow of plenty was known for the copious amount of milk she yielded that tasted like nectar.

The wife of the Vasu Dyou looked longingly at the cow and told her husband, 'I have a friend who is the daughter of King Ushinara. I want to gift this cow to her so she can drink its milk and be free from illness and ageing. Get me this cow.'

Without considering the consequences, Dyou and his brothers stole the cow. When Vasishta realised the cow was missing, he used his powers to find out who had done it.

He angrily cursed the Vasus, saying, 'You who have stolen my cow are undeserving of being celestials. I curse all of you to be reborn as humans.'

The Vasus returned the cow and pleaded for forgiveness.

Vasishta refused but agreed that seven of them would be freed quickly. Dyou, the mastermind, would suffer a long human life.

The curse of Vasishta thus caused the Vasus to be born on earth.

Meanwhile, another significant incident took place in the abode of Brahma.

In Brahma's court, a gust of wind displaced Ganga's garments. While others looked away, Mahabhisha stared.

Seeing this, Brahma was furious. He cursed Mahabhisha, saying, 'For this sinful act of yours, you will be reborn on earth and only then return to this world.'

Mahabhisha went away sadly, preparing to leave the world of the celestials. Ganga was also disturbed and went away from there. She then saw the Vasus, who had been thrown out of the celestial world.

The Vasus pleaded with Ganga to be their mother on Earth.

Ganga agreed to this, and the Vasus left, preparing to be reborn on earth.

Ganga then assumed the form of a beautiful woman and approached the great King Pratipa of Hastinapura, intending to fulfil her promise to the Vasus.

'O great king. Accept me as your wife,' said Ganga and sat on the right thigh of Pratipa.

Pratipa said, 'You have sat on my right thigh, which is reserved for daughters and daughters-in-law to sit. I will offer you the status of my daughter-in-law.'

Ganga agreed and promised to bear a son who would bring glory to the Kuru race.

Pratipa had a son named Shantanu, who grew up to be a wise and valorous prince. Pratipa summoned Shantanu when we came of marriageable age and told him, 'A beautiful lady will approach you and seek to be your wife. Accept her without questioning her.'

Pratipa then installed Shantanu on the throne of Hastinapura and retired to the forests.

One day, when Shantanu went hunting, he saw a

beautiful lady seated near the Ganga River. The king of Hastinapura fell in love with her just by seeing her beautiful form. Remembering his father's words, Shantanu went to the beautiful lady and proposed marriage to her.

She agreed to marry him on the condition that he never question her actions.

Shantanu agreed to her condition and married the lady, who was none other than Ganga. He led a happy life with her, and soon she was pregnant. When she delivered the baby, she left the palace at night, holding the baby in her arms. A surprised Shantanu followed her to see where she was going.

She went to the river and drowned the baby in the river, even as Shantanu watched on in shock. Shantanu was outraged and was tempted to grab her and question her for drowning his child. Remembering her condition and his father's advice, he kept quiet and pretended as though he did not know what happened.

Soon, his wife became pregnant and delivered a baby boy yet again. In the same way as the previous time, she drowned the baby in the river. Shantanu had no option but to keep quiet. She drowned seven sons as Shantanu remained silent.

She then gave birth to an eighth child and, as usual, went to drown the child. This time, Shantanu could not control himself. He wanted an heir, but his wife was killing their children. This time, he would not allow her to drown the baby. He grabbed her arm and prevented her from drowning the baby.

'Enough! I will not let you kill another son.'

His wife replied, 'Since you stopped me, I will keep this child. I am Ganga, and your sons were the cursed Vasus. This one, Devavratha, will bring you pride.'

With these words, Ganga vanished with the child, leaving Shantanu heartbroken.

Years later, Ganga returned with their son, Devavratha, now a skilled warrior trained by Parashurama. Shantanu made him crown prince.

Later, Devavratha would become Bheeshma, and he would ensure Shantanu married again.

Upon Shantanu's death, he returned to his celestial form as Mahabhisha, while Devavratha, the eighth Vasu, fulfilled his destiny on Earth.

He lived a life of Dharma as the protector of Hastinapura. His good deeds ensured his father reached Heaven. Finally, after the Kurukshetra war ended, he gave up his life and returned to the world of Vasus in his original form of Dyou.

■

The story of the Vasus, Mahabhisha, and the curse that caused them to be born on earth is narrated in the *Adi Parva* of the Mahabharata. The story of Bheeshma having to live long and being unmarried is explained by this story of how he was cursed by Vashishta.

17

The Curse That Changed History

The King of Hastinapura stood ramrod straight in his chariot as it raced through the forest. He was in the mood to hunt and looked around for animals to bring down. Pandu, though not the eldest, ruled due to his brother's blindness and proved his worth through conquests. Exultant after his victories, he celebrated by indulging in his favourite pastime of hunting.

He particularly loved hunting deer. As his chariot moved, he spotted a mating stag and doe and aimed. He released five arrows that struck the stag and doe. While the doe died immediately, the stag went through a death struggle. Even as it struggled, it spoke with a human voice, shocking Pandu.

The stag was not a deer but was a sage mating with his wife in the guise of a deer.

O arrogant king, you slew me as I united with my wife, ending my lineage. I curse you—if you mate, you and your wife shall die.

Shocked and despairing, Pandu renounced his throne and retreated to the forest with his wives.

Later on, he learned of a boon his wife Kunti had from a sage. Using the boon, Pandu had three sons by Kunti and two by Madri. The sons were born by a union between his wives and the Gods.

Pandu was now happy. He had five sons who would continue his lineage. One day, as he walked with Madri in the rain, desire overcame him.

Overcome by passion, Pandu forgot the curse. The moment he embraced Madri, he fell dead.

Pandu was dead. Grieving, Madri immolated herself on his pyre.

The sage Kindama's curse had come true. Pandu and his wife were dead, in the same way as the sage and his wife died. Pandu left the world, leaving his widow Kunti, to bring up his five young sons.

■

The curse, as narrated in the Adi Parva, forced Pandu to renounce the throne, paving the way for Dhritarashtra's rule.

Dhritarashtra's rule enabled Duryodhana's rise, leading to the Kurukshetra war and the destruction of the Kuru race.

Had Pandu not been cursed, he would have remained king, changing history. There are parallels between Pandu and Rama's father Dasharatha. Both of them killed an innocent person while hunting and were subject to curses.

Pandu's curse caused his death and left his sons orphaned and at the mercy of their uncle and cousins. Dasharatha's curse left him a broken man separated from his beloved son, Rama. The desire to hunt and kill animals wantonly resulted in the death of two great kings and curses that would change the course of events.

Hunting is mentioned as a vice. In the Mahabharata's *Aranyaka Parva*, Krishna tells Yudhishtira that four things arise from a desire that leads to loss of prosperity. The four things were gambling, hunting, drinking, and desiring women. Hunting is thus mentioned as an evil that would lead to loss of prosperity. Even though they knew this, kings continued to hunt, and as it happened to Pandu and Dasharatha, they became the victims of curses.

Another interesting aspect is the killing of animals that are mating. In the Ramayana, the killing of mating herons makes Valmiki curse a hunter. In the Mahabharata, Pandu's killing of the mating deer causes him to receive a curse that leads to his death.

18

The Curse That Led to Duryodhana's Death

Dhritarashtra was deeply troubled, knowing he had acted against *Dharma*. His blind love for his son had led to a situation where he had unjustly sent the sons of his late brother into exile.

Because of Duryodhana's greed, the Pandavas lived in exile like ascetics. Dhritarashtra had now realised that his fear of his son's threats to kill himself had led to this situation.

Dhritarashtra dreaded the Pandavas' return and the war it could bring.

Vyasa arrived, and Dhritarashtra pleaded, 'Advise my son to make peace with the Pandavas.'

'I will not do this, but the sage Maitreya will,' said Vyasa. 'He has spent time with the Pandavas and seen them in exile. He will advise your son on what to do.'

After Vyasa left, Sage Maitreya arrived and was greeted by Duryodhana

Maitreya warned, 'Do not envy your cousins. You cannot win against them, so make peace and live as brothers.'

Fuming, Duryodhana ignored the sage, drawing patterns on the ground

Maitreya warned again, 'You cannot defeat the Pandavas, especially with Krishna by their side. Make peace.

Furious, Duryodhana slapped his thigh in defiance.
Seeing Duryodhana's arrogance, the sage rose in anger.
You have sown war and will reap its fruits. I curse you—
Bheema will break your thighs and kill you.

The sage left, and Dhritarashtra trembled, knowing his worst fears would soon unfold.

■

Maitreya's curse, found in the Aranyaka Parva, sealed Duryodhana's fate.

Bheema vowed to break Duryodhana's thigh after he insulted Draupadi, and Maitreya's curse ensured it came true.

The sage's words were never false. Thirteen years later, Bheema shattered Duryodhana's thigh, leaving him to die a painful death.

19

The Son Who Saved the Father Who Cursed Him

Sage Uddalaka, pleased with his disciple Kahoda's wisdom, gave him his daughter Sujata in marriage.

Kahoda lived happily with Sujata, and soon, she became pregnant. Sujata was interested in the scriptures. Kahoda would chant the Vedic hymns as Sujata listened to them. The child inside Sujata's womb also heard and understood the hymns.

One day, as Kahoda taught his students, a feeble voice interrupted, 'Father, your hymn is incorrect.'

Everyone looked around in surprise. Kahoda understood what had happened. His unborn son had spoken from his wife's womb and had pointed out a mistake he had committed. Kahoda was furious that his son had caused him embarrassment before his students. He cursed his unborn son, saying, 'You will be born with defects in your body because you dared insult me.'

The child was born with eight defects that made his body crooked. He was named Ashtavakra. Even before Ashtavakra was born, Kahoda had gone to King Janaka's court and never returned.

Uddalaka then learned that when Kahoda reached Janaka's palace, he was challenged by the eminent scholar Bandi for a debate. The condition of the debate was that the loser would have to drown in the river. Kahoda lost the debate and was drowned in the waters.

Ashtavakra grew up believing Uddalaka was his father. One day, he learned Uddalaka was not his father but his grandfather. His brother Shwetaketu was seated on his father's lap. When Ashtavakra tried to climb onto Uddalaka's lap, Shwetaketu pushed him away. That was when Ashtavakra learned Shwetaketu was not his brother, but his uncle and that Uddalaka was his mother's father.

Sujata revealed how Bandi had defeated and drowned Kahoda.

Ashtavakra, who was ten years old, was well-learned in the scriptures. He decided to go to the court of King Janaka and challenge Bandi. Shwetaketu accompanied him on this journey. The king met the young boy and was impressed by his wisdom. He agreed to allow the young boy to debate with the veteran scholar Bandi.

Ashtavakra then stunned everyone by defeating Bandi in the debate. He then demanded that Bandi be given the same punishment that his father Uddalaka was given.

Bandi revealed he was Varuna's son and had sent the sages to aid a sacrifice, not kill them.

Bandi then entered the water to return to the abode of his father. Soon, Kahoda and the other sages who had been defeated by Bandi in debates came out of the water.

Kahoda embraced his son and said, 'O son, I am such an arrogant man that I cursed a wise child like you to be born with defects. You have repaid my curse by challenging and defeating the great Bandi, allowing me to be reunited with my family. You are a blessed child. Despite all your defects, you will grow to be an outstanding scholar whose teachings will be remembered forever.'

Kahoda and Ashtavakra happily hurried home to meet Sujata and Uddalaka.

■

The story of Ashtavakra being cursed by his father and the incidents that occurred therein is narrated in the Aranyaka Parva of the Mahabharata. Indra instructs the sage Lomasha to take the Pandavas on a pilgrimage while they await Arjuna's return from Indraloka.

During the pilgrimage, Lomasha shows the Pandavas the ashrama of the sage Shvetaketu. He then narrates the story of Ashtavakra.

Ashtavakra's meeting with King Janaka, and their philosophical discourse is legendary. This is recorded in the form of the Ashtavakra Geeta, a famous treatise that is popular even today.

20

How Did Bheema Redeem Kubera's Curse?

The Pushpaka Vimana soared in the sky with Kubera seated on the throne at the centre. Next to him was his friend, Maniman. Kubera and his advisers were on their way to Kushavati to attend the meeting of the council of celestials.

As they passed over the Yamuna, they saw the sage Agastya standing on a rock in the middle of the waters, performing penances. Maniman who had become insolent due to his powers as a Yaksha, sniggered seeing the sage.

Suddenly, Maniman did something that shocked Kubera. Even before Kubera could realise what had happened, Maniman leaned out from the Pushpaka Vimana and spat at the sage. The saliva spat out by Maniman went racing towards the ground and landed on Agastya's head.

The sage looked up and, seeing the Vimana, glowered at it. The sage's gaze was so intense that the aerial vehicle failed to move forward and came crashing down, landing on the water.

Agastya was wild with anger. Turning to Maniman, he said, 'You deserve to be punished for your evil act. You no longer will remain a yaksha. I curse you to become a rakshasa. O Kubera, this happened in your presence, and so the effect of my curse will also affect you. After many years, this rakshasa will be killed by a human. On that day, this curse will be redeemed.'

The moment the curse was uttered, the handsome Maniman became a huge and ugly ogre. With a heavy heart, Kubera left Maniman in the Gandhamadana Mountains, asking him to guard his lake in the mountains.

Kubera waited for hundreds of years for the curse to be redeemed. During this period, he lost his brilliance due to the effect of Agastya's curse.

One day, Kubera's men came running to his palace. 'The lake, the mountains, a massacre has occurred,' they shouted in confusion.

'Calm down,' said the Lord of the Yakshas. 'Don't talk all together. Only one of you talk.'

'Maniman is dead, my Lord,' said a guard.

'What!' said Kubera, getting up from his throne. 'Maniman is dead? How did it happen? Tell me fast?'

'A mighty human warrior climbed the mountains and wanted to take the lotuses from the lake. When our guards objected, he fought with us. He has a mighty club and used it to clobber our guards. When Maniman tried to stop him, the human smashed his head into pieces and killed him.'

Kubera immediately climbed into his Pushpaka Vimana and left towards the lake. There, he saw the mighty warrior resting with the bloodstained club lying by his side. Surrounding him were other humans.

Kubera recognised them instantly. They were the Pandavas with their wife, Draupadi. Seeing Kubera, they came to him and sought his blessings.

Bheema bowed before Kubera.

Kubera smiled and said, 'O Yudhishtira, I know you are angry with Bheema for causing this slaughter, but do not blame him. Bheema has done me a favour by killing Maniman and the other guards. Maniman was under a curse and by killing him, Bheema released him from the curse. The curse on me has also been released thanks to Bheema.'

Kubera blessed Bheema by touching him on the head. 'You have unknowingly helped me. But you need to control your violent behaviour. Yudhishtira, try to control your brother's behaviour so he does not create more violence in these mountains. You can stay here with your family for as long as you want. Your brother Arjuna is in Indraloka and has obtained celestial weapons. He will soon be with you.'

With these words, Kubera blessed the Pandavas and left from there on his Pushpaka Vimana, relieved that the curse of Agastya had been redeemed.

The incident of Bheema killing Maniman and redeeming Agastya's curse is part of the *Aranyaka Parva* of the Mahabharata. Arjuna leaves for Indra's abode to get celestial weapons. Unable to live without him, the Pandavas go to the Gandhamadhana mountains to welcome him when he returns.

One day, Draupadi saw an exotic lotus and wished to have more such flowers. Eager to please her, Bheema sets out to climb the mountains and reaches Kubera's lake, where the lotuses grew. He then killed the guards, including Maniman, and claimed the lotuses. Worried that Bheema had not returned, Yudhishtira summoned Bheema's son, the rakshasa Ghatotkacha, and asked him to take them to the mountains.

When they reached the mountains, Yudhishtira rebuked Bheema for indulging in such killing and destruction. Just then, Kubera arrived there and thanked them for relieving him of the curse. He granted them permission to stay there. The Pandavas stayed there for a while, enjoying the beauty of nature until Arjuna returned to rejoin them.

21

The Curse That Made a King Turn into a Serpent

Nahusha, a mere mortal, had become the Lord of the three worlds and was now seated on the throne of Indra.

It was a dream for every king to gain the position of Indra. For this, they would perform sacrifices that Indra would try to stop. Nahusha did not perform any sacrifice but was invited by the Gods themselves to occupy the position of Indra. He could never forget that day when the Gods had come to him.

'All the Gods and holy sages are here before me. What an honour! Agni, Vayu, Varuna, Yama, all the celestials have come to meet me, the king of the earth. I am truly blessed.'

'O Nahusha, we need your help,' said Agni.

'We are in a difficult situation,' said Vayu. 'Indra is missing, and his throne is empty.'

'After killing the demon Vritra, Indra was depressed. He had killed Viswarupa, a Brahmana who was the son of Twashtra. An angry Twashtra then created Vritra, leading to a terrible war that Indra eventually won. Afflicted with the sin of killing a Brahmana, Indra has gone into hiding and is carrying out austerities. We now need a king to rule Heaven,' said Yama.

'That is why we have come to you,' said Varuna. 'You are

a great king, known for your valour, wisdom, and virtuous behaviour. So we want you to rule over Heaven until Indra returns.'

Nahusha hesitated, but the Gods granted him a powerful gaze that would control all who looked into his eyes.

Drunk with power, Nahusha ruled Heaven, his gaze making all bow before him.

Seeing Shachi's empty throne, Nahusha desired Indra's wife as his queen.

'Why is Shachi not here? She is the wife of Indra, and I am Indra. She should be here,' declared Nahusha.

He then sent Agni and the other gods to Shachi to bring her to the palace.

Shachi sought Brihaspati's help to protect her honour and loyalty to Indra.

'Do not worry, Shachi,' said Brihaspathi. 'I will help you. It is time for the arrogant Nahusha, who is drunk with power, to be taught a lesson. Tell him you will accept him only if he comes to you in a palanquin drawn by the seven holy sages.'

Shachi bowed to Brihaspathi and went to meet Nahusha. The new Lord of Heaven was smitten seeing the beauty of Shachi. 'Why do you not come to me, O beautiful one?' he asked. 'I am the most powerful being on earth. Your husband, Indra, has run away like a coward. I will protect you, be mine.'

Shachi, with her eyes downcast, told Nahusha, 'I want you to come to me in a vehicle that befits your might. Come to my palace in a palanquin drawn by the seven holy sages. I will then be yours.'

An arrogant Nahusha laughed, promising to come to her in such a palanquin.

He then summoned the seven sages. Looking him in

the eyes made their knees shake; such was the power he had in his eyes.

'You will carry me in a palanquin and take me to the palace of Shachi,' ordered Nahusha.

Humiliated and depressed at the disrespect shown by Nahusha but left with no option, the sages carried Nahusha in a palanquin.

Nahusha was delighted. Even the great sages could not say no to him. Soon, Shachi would be his. He would then rule the world with the lovely Shachi as his queen.

The sages then set out to implement Brihaspathi's plan. They questioned Nahusha on certain mantras told by Brahma and asked him if the mantras were correct. The vain Nahusha replied in the negative. The sages then began to argue with Nahusha, making him angry. He then kicked out with his foot, hitting Agastya in the head.

Without turning back, Agastya declared loudly, 'O arrogant Nahusha, the holy sages are equivalent to Brahma, and you make us carry you around. You now dare to touch me with your feet. I curse you, Nahusha, to lose all your powers and merits and become a snake. You will roam the forests of the earth for ten thousand years. You will be freed when the most virtuous of your descendants meets you.'

The moment the curse was uttered, Nahusha turned into an enormous snake. Screaming in shock, he fell from the heavens and landed on earth. The snake roamed the earth for thousands of years, waiting for salvation.

One day, the snake spotted a mighty man walking through the forest. Nahusha grabbed the mighty warrior, who fiercely grappled with the snake. Nahusha was amazed by the strength of the man, but finally subdued him.

After some time, the man's brother came there.

'O mighty snake. I am Yudhishtira, and the man in your grip is my brother Bheema. We mean no harm to anyone and are spending our life in exile in the forest. Please release my brother.'

Nahusha then realised that Yudhishtira was the one who would release him from his curse. He tested Yudhishtira by questioning him about intelligence, consciousness, and other topics. Yudhishtira answered all the snake's questions.

His interaction with the virtuous Yudhishtira had freed him from the curse. Nahusha revealed his identity, blessed Yudhishtira, and ascended to Heaven, freed from the curse.

■

The story of Nahusha's curse is narrated in the Udyoga and Aranyaka Parvas of the Mahabharata. The curse is narrated in its entirety in the *Udyoga Parva* of the Mahabharata. Shalya narrates the story of Nahusha to Yudhishtira and his brothers. The incident of the meeting between Yudhishtira and the snake is a part of the *Aranyaka Parva* of the Mahabharata.

There is a popular story about Agastya's curse, found in some versions of the Mahabharata. According to this version, Agastya was slowing down the movement of the palanquin because he was shorter than the other sages. So the angry Nahusha kicked him and said, 'Sarpa, sarpa' (which means move fast). An angry Agastya cursed him, saying, 'Sarpo bhava' (become a snake). This version is, however, not found in the major editions of the Mahabharata.

Nahusha's story illustrates how arrogance and misuse of power lead to downfall.

Many stories about Nahusha can be found. It is said that Nahusha is the son-in-law of Shiva. A fact not known to many is about Ashok Sundari, the daughter of Shiva and Parvati. The Padma Purana narrates how Parvati got a daughter from the Kalpavriksha tree who she named Ashoka Sundari. Nahusha later killed a demon called Hunda, who had troubled Ashok Sundari. He then married her, becoming the son-in-law of Shiva and Shakti.

Even though he had such an illustrious background, arrogance led to his downfall. The story is relevant because Duryodhana's arrogance was similar to Nahusha's. He was so arrogant that he refused to heed the advice of his parents, Bheeshma, Parashurama, Narada, and even Krishna. Finally, his arrogance led to his gruesome death in a terrible war that led to devastation.

22

The Curses That Doomed Karna

'I am tired, Karna,' said Parashurama, sitting beside Karna and wiping sweat from his brow. He had just returned from a visit to a nearby village in the scorching sun.

Karna ran and got water for his teacher, who drank it gratefully.

'Rest for some time, sire,' said Karna to his teacher, whose ashrama he had lived in for the past few years to master the art of weaponry.

'I think I will do that. My body is aching, and a quick nap will re-energise me.'

Karna sat down and invited his teacher to lie down on his lap. Parashurama placed his head on his student's lap and lay down. Karna cradled his teacher's head, using his palms like a pillow. Within seconds, Parashurama was fast asleep. Karna looked at his teacher's calm face and smiled.

The best decision he had taken in his life was to come to Parashurama's ashrama. After Drona denied the knowledge of the higher Brahmastra, an angry Karna stormed out of Drona's hermitage. The favouritism shown by Drona to Arjuna deeply upset him.

Knowing Parashurama would not deny knowledge to a Brahmana, Karna disguised himself as one to gain admission.

He came to Mahendragiri dressed like a Brahmana, and gained admission by telling a lie. Being already skilled in archery, he was a quick learner.

Parashurama was pleased with Karna's dedication and granted him the coveted Brahmastra, along with the knowledge of many celestial weapons. Impressed by his devotion, Parashurama gifted him the powerful Bhargavastra, a weapon of his own creation.

Karna smiled in joy at seeing the serene face of his teacher lying on his lap. His stay at the ashrama was nearly over. He would go back and prove to the world that he was now the greatest warrior in the world. Neither Arjuna nor Drona could stop his rise now.

Karna felt a sharp pain as a bee stung his thigh; its sting lodged deep in his flesh.

Enduring the pain silently, Karna refused to disturb his sleeping teacher.

The pain intensified with each passing moment as the bee struggled to pull out its sting. Eventually, the sting broke off, embedding itself deep within the flesh. The bee fell lifeless, leaving behind torn skin and oozing blood.

The blood spread, staining Karna's white garment crimson. Though tempted to remove the sting, Karna knew it would disturb Parashurama's rest. Enduring excruciating pain, tears flowed down his cheeks, but he did not flinch. When Parashurama awoke, his gaze fell on the dried tears and the bloodstained thigh. Understanding the situation, he saw the dead bee and anger blazed in his eyes. 'Karna, you have deceived me. How could you do this?' Struggling to his feet, Karna bowed his head. 'What happened, sire?' Parashurama pointed to the wound. 'That pain would make anyone cry out, but you didn't. No Brahmana could bear such agony. Who are you, Karna? Why did you deceive me?'

Karna stood shamefacedly before his teacher, 'Forgive me, revered Rama. Indeed, I am not a Brahmana. I am the son of a Suta. I had no option but to lie to you since I was desperate to be your student. I have been a dedicated student and respect you more than anyone in the world. Please forgive the lie I told you.'

'I agree that you have been a good student. But I cannot tolerate lies. You must pay for this. Leave my ashrama immediately. For cheating your teacher, you deserve to be cursed. This is my curse, Karna. When the time comes when you will need the Brahmastra the most, you will forget the ability to summon it.'

With these words, Parashurama walked away from there. A distraught Karna realised he had no option but to leave the ashrama.

He walked away dejectedly, cursing his fate. As he roamed directionless, Karna heard movement behind a bush. Instinct took over. He swiftly fixed an arrow and released it. The arrow shot through the bush, striking its target.

But instead of a leopard's roar, Karna heard the mournful mooing of a dying cow.

The shocked Karna ran to the bush and pushed it back. He saw a cow lying dead behind the bush. Karna dropped his bow, distraught at the fact that he had committed the terrible sin of killing a cow.

'You vile man,' said a voice from behind him.

Karna looked back and saw a Brahmana come running towards him. Falling on the ground, he held the cow's head and cried.

'You evil man, you killed my poor cow. The helpless thing was incapable of harming you, and yet you killed it to show off your might. What a wicked man you are. The sin of killing a cow will destroy you. I curse you, arrogant warrior. One day, you will be in the same position as my cow, helpless and without weapons. In the same way you killed my cow, a warrior greater than you will kill you.'

Karna fell to the ground, breaking down. It was the most terrible day of his life. He had been cursed twice, and the curses had doomed him. He wondered when the day would come when the curses would destroy him.

The story of Karna being cursed is famous and well-known by everyone who knows the story of the Mahabharata. The curses came true on the seventeenth day of the Kurukshetra War. During the decisive battle with Arjuna, Karna's chariot was stuck in the earth and could not dislodge the stuck wheel despite his best efforts.

That was when Parashurama's curse came true, and Karna could not remember the use of the Brahmastra taught by his teacher. Arjuna then destroyed Karna's bow. He stood helpless on the battlefield, like the cow he had killed. Just as he killed the cow, so did Arjuna kill Karna.

■

This story appears in the Karna Parva of the Mahabharata, where Karna recounts it to Shalya, his charioteer for the day. He reveals that Indra, disguised as an insect, bit him to expose his identity, leading to Parashurama's curse.

The Brahmana's curse is mentioned in the Shanti Parva, narrated by Narada to Yudhishtira. It foretells that Karna's chariot would be trapped when his head would be cut off.

These curses severely impacted Karna. As a result, Bheeshma labelled him as an Ardharatha or half a warrior, a humiliation that made Karna refuse to fight under Bheeshma.

The curses dangled over Karna's neck like a sword. Finally, he lost his life with Arjuna cutting off his head. Parashurama was not particularly angry with Karna, and his curse did not cause him to forget all his weapons. He only forgot the use of the higher Brahmastra, and used other weapons against Arjuna.

While the *Shalya Parva* says that the insect that bit Karna was Indra in the form of a bee, the *Shanti Parva* has another version. There, it is said that it was a worm that bit Karna. The worm was a rakshasa named Praggritsa who had been cursed by Bhrigu.

In another popular story, Karna caused a child to drop ghee on the earth. Karna squeezed the earth to extract the ghee and make the child happy. The earth then cursed Karna, saying one day, his chariot would be stuck in the earth, and he would not be able to pull out the wheel. This curse is a folktale and not mentioned in the Mahabharata.

23

The Curse That Made Shikhandi a Man

The cry of a newborn usually brings joy, but not for King Drupada. His heart was heavy with tension as he anxiously awaited the midwife's news. Despite clinging to hope, he knew Shiva's words would not be false.

The midwife came out, holding the baby in her arms.

'It's a girl,' she said, her eyes downcast, knowing that her master wanted a boy.

Drupada's shoulders sagged. Unlike most kings who desired an heir, he wished for a son who would grow into a warrior capable of defeating his arch-enemy, Drona.

Taking a deep breath, Drupada looked at his child. He had come to a decision. He kissed the child on its forehead and told the midwife, 'I am so happy I have a son.'

'My Lord,' said the midwife, confusion writ on her face. 'This is a girl.'

'I know it, you know it, and my wife knows it. No one else will know it. You will be with my wife and bring up this girl as a boy. You will now go and announce to the world that a son has been born to the king. I will bring up this child as a boy. He will be known as Shikhandi.'

The scared midwife nodded her head in fear. She was not foolish to disobey a royal order.

The girl, Shikhandini, was brought up as a boy. Drupada kept the truth about the child's gender a secret. To the world, the prince was Shikhandi. The child grew up to be skilled in the arts, and Drupada sent the child to Drona to be trained. Even Drona was fooled and never realised his student was a girl.

One day, the queen came to Drupada with a worried expression.

'What happened, my dear?' asked Drupada.

'Our child has matured into a woman. How will we conceal her gender now?'

Drupada sighed, 'Lord Shiva appeared in my dream and foretold that my daughter would one day become a man. I have raised her as a boy, trusting in Mahadeva's words, which can never be false.

We must continue this path. Let us find a wife for my son and keep up the charade until Mahadeva reveals the way.'

Drupada's wife agreed and took great pains to hide the fact that Shikhandi had blossomed into a woman. Soon, Shikhandi was of marriageable age. The Dasharna king, Hiranayavarma, sent a proposal for his daughter to marry Shikhandi.

Drupada went ahead with the marriage, hoping desperately for a miracle. He wanted this marriage because an alliance with the powerful Hiranyavarma was good for his kingdom. He also was confident that Lord Shiva would offer a solution to this problem.

Soon after marriage, Shikhandi's wife came to know that her husband was a woman and not a man. Shocked, she confided in her maid, who spread the news to the royal palace at Dasharna.

Hiranyavarma was furious and sent a message to Drupada. The messenger came to Drupada's chambers and revealed the message, 'King of Panchala, you have deceived me. I will not forgive this deception. I will destroy you and your kingdom.'

This news disturbed Drupada. His spies told him that Hiranyavarma was assembling a vast army, ready to march to Panchala. Drupada and his wife wept over their fate. Shikhandini heard her parents crying and knew that she was to blame.

Resolved to end the turmoil, Shikhandini set off to the forest to end her life. There, she encountered Sthuna, a yaksha who ruled the woods. Intrigued, Sthuna watched the woman dressed as a man, curious to learn why she sought death.

Sthuna asked Shikhandini, 'Why do you want to end your life? Being a woman, why are you dressed like a man? Tell me about your problem, and I will try to help you.'

Shikhandini then told the entire story and explained how her father was in danger of being killed by the Dasharna king.

Sthuna said, 'I am Kubera's follower and have divine powers. I will help you. I will exchange my genitals with you, so I will become a woman, and you will be a man. You can then go back and convince the world that you are a man. Once Hiranyavarma is satisfied, we will re-exchange our genders.'

Shikhandini was happy with the yaksha's and thanked him profusely. Accordingly, they exchanged their genders and Shikhandini became a man.

He went and told his father everything. Overjoyed,

Drupada sent a message to Hiranyavarma saying that his son was a man, and the king should trust him. Hiranayavarma rushed to Panchala. He asked his advisors to physically examine Shikhandi. When they examined the prince of Panchala, they found he had all the organs of a man.

They reported this to Hiranyavarma, who was happy. The king returned satisfied, and all was well in both the kingdoms.

Meanwhile, Kubera had come to earth. He was surprised to see that Sthuna was avoiding him. He then summoned Sthuna's aide, who revealed the truth. Kubera was furious, and ordered Sthuna to be brought before him.

'How dare you change your gender without my permission?' said Kubera in anger. 'I made you the Lord of this forest, and you have betrayed me by changing your gender in this way. I curse you, Sthuna to be a woman forever. You will not have the power to exchange your gender again.'

Sthuna then became a woman permanently, while Shikhandi became a man forever. Shikhandi was happy with this news since now he would live like a man and be the son his father wanted. Sthuna was terribly unhappy and went to meet his Lord.

Sthuna fell at Kubera's feet and pleaded, 'Forgive me, Lord. I do not wish to be a woman. Please withdraw your curse and bless me.'

Kubera said, 'I cannot withdraw my curse. You will continue to be a woman. Shikhandi is a warrior and faces the risk of death in war. The day he dies, you will become a man again.'

A satisfied Sthuna returned to his forest, eagerly awaiting Shikhandi's death. Many years later, Shikhandi fought in the

Kurukshetra war. The night after the war was over, he was killed by Drona's son Ashwatthama in a surprise attack. The moment Shikhandi died, Sthuna once again became a man and was happy to regain his original form.

■

The story of Shikhandini becoming a man is found in the *Bheeshma Parva*. This story is narrated by Bheeshma to Duryodhana. The sage Narada had told the story of Shikhandini becoming Shikhandi to Bheeshma. While the story of Amba being reborn as Shikhandi is well-known, the story involving the yaksha Sthuna is not so famous. This story gives a logical explanation for why Bheeshma refused to fight Shikhandi.

The conventional explanation is that Bheeshma refused to fight Shikhandi because he was Amba in his previous birth. Amba was a princess who had taken an oath to be reborn and kill Bheeshma in her next life. Shikhandi was Amba reborn, but this was not why Bheeshma avoided him. Bheeshma knew Shikhandi was a woman Shikhandini and hence avoided fighting with him. On the tenth day of the Kurukshetra War, Arjuna placed Shikhandi before him. He then brought down Bheeshma, ending his reign as Kaurava commander.

24

The Curse That Made Chandra Wax and Wane

Prajapati Daksha, the Lord of all the worlds, was mad with anger. This was the second time his daughters had come to him to complain. He could not believe that Chandra had failed to heed his words.

'Father, you ruined our lives by marrying us to Chandra,' cried his daughters, the nakshatras. 'You got all twenty-seven of us married to Chandra so we would live together happily. You promised happiness in the abode of the moon, but he ignores us all except Rohini.'

Outraged, Daksha fumed, 'Chandra dares to defy my words. I advised him to treat you all equally, yet he continues to neglect you.'

'Even after complaining to you, there is no use. Chandra does not even look at us. He is so enamoured of Rohini it is as though we don't exist. We do not want to go back to Chandraloka. There is no use staying there. We are all dejected with life.'

Daksha was wild with rage at hearing his daughter's words. He then uttered a curse, 'I hereby curse Chandra that he would be affected by consumption and would waste away. He would decay progressively day and day and end up being completely wasted away. This is the punishment he will suffer for disregarding me.'

Daksha's curse left Chandra in disarray. He began to waste away suffering from the terrible disease of tuberculosis. His radiance was affected and started to diminish. Soon, the moon's light began to reduce on earth and the earth started to become completely dark. The absence of the moon affected plants and animals. Life on earth became difficult.

The Gods who came to know of this were worried. If Chandra wasted away completely, there would be no moonlight on earth. There would be eternal darkness, and many herbs and plants would not grow. Animal life would be affected. It would cause widespread chaos.

The Gods went to meet Daksha and pleaded with him, 'O son of Brahma, your curse is causing difficulty to the world. So take back your curse. Chandra has been chastised and has realised his mistake. Forgive him and save the world.'

'A curse once uttered cannot be undone. However, if Chandra agrees to treat my daughters equally, I will modify it. He will continue to decay but will regain his brilliance once fully diminished. This cycle will repeat every month: fifteen days of waning followed by fifteen days of waxing.'

Daksha then told the Gods, 'For my words to come true, Chandra has to first wash off his sins. He has to go to the Prabhasa Kshetra and bathe in the Saraswati River to cleanse himself of his sins.

Chandra then went to Prabhasa and bathed in the Saraswati. He once again started to grow in brilliance and reached his full effulgence. But again, he started to weaken and decay. This continued month after month and soon became normal. The world was quickly adjusted to this cycle of the moon's waxing and waning.

■

The story of the curse that led to the waxing and waning of the moon is found in the *Shalya Parva* of the Mahabharata. Just before the final duel between Bheema and Duryodhana starts, Krishna's brother Balarama arrives after completing a pilgrimage. Vaishampayana, who is narrating the Mahabharata to Emperor Janmejaya, provides details of Balarama's pilgrimage.

Balarama commences his pilgrimage from Prabhasa. Vaishampayana then narrated the curse to Chandra and how it was modified by Chandra visiting Prabhasa.

The moon's waxing and waning is the subject of many tales. A popular story is that the moon was cursed by Ganesha for mocking him. It is believed that Ganesha modified his curse to allow the moon to wax and wane. There is a belief that whoever sees the moon on the day of Ganesha Chaturthi will suffer infamy due to the effect of this curse.

The Mahabharata has a different explanation for the waxing and waning of the moon illustrated in the story narrated above.

25

Gandhari Curses Krishna

Every time Duryodhana sought his mother's blessings, Gandhari would say, 'May the righteous win.'

He would ask his mother, 'Why don't you bless me with victory?'

Gandhari would not respond but caress her eldest son's head.

Now, on the bloodstained ground of Kurukshetra, Gandhari caressed his head once more—this time, he did not respond. Her son lay dead before her.

Maybe she should have wished him victory. Why did she ask for the victory of the righteous ones? In her heart, she knew her son represented all that was unrighteous. That is why he lost the war and lay dead on the battleground.

His body was anointed daily with sandalwood and fragrances now smelt of decayed flesh. Vultures and jackals now ravaged the body covered by jewellery and armour. Weeping piteously, Gandhari cradled her son's head on her lap.

She had a hundred sons born after great difficulty, and now every single one of them was dead. She had been tempted to curse Yudhishtira but controlled herself, but she was now losing control.

Her grief was replaced with fury. She was angry with many people but more so with herself. Her son may have survived had she corrected him when he went on the wrong path.

With her husband seated next to her, holding her hand, she cried until every drop of tear had been exhausted.

She looked up and, even though she was blindfolded, sensed the presence of Krishna standing next to her.

'Look, Madhava, see my son Duryodhana. He lies dead. See how his widow weeps. Look around you at all the dead warriors. Look at my daughter Dusshala, who cries because she is widowed. Look at the gentle Uttara who weeps at the loss of her valorous husband, Abhimanyu. Look around you and see all those who died. Kings who lived in palaces now lie on the ground, their bodies ravaged by carrion eaters.'

Gandhari got up, holding the ground for support. Her blindfolded eyes looked at Krishna, and she said,

'Madhusudana, so many people died, and you watched them die. You are the Lord of this world and could have easily stopped this destruction. You did not lift a finger to stop this massacre.'

Gandhari took a deep breath and pointed at Krishna. 'Vaasudeva, you are responsible for the destruction of the Kuru clan. I curse you, Krishna. Thirty-six years from now, your Yadava clan will destroy itself, just as the Kurus did. Their women will mourn their dead, just as my daughters-in-law mourn today. As my son lies dead before me, so shall you meet a tragic end, dying a horrible death.'

Gandhari's words stunned the Pandavas, who looked on in a state of shock not knowing what to do. Having uttered the curse, Gandhari fell on the ground crying again, her husband vainly trying to console her.

Krishna smiled at Gandhari. 'Get up, Gandhari. Do not grieve anymore. You are responsible for all that has happened. You ignored the evil behaviour of your son. When your son harassed the Pandavas, you did not lift a finger to stop your vile son. Now, why do you blame me for what happened? Your curse is unjustified, but I accept it. What you have said has already been ordained and will happen.'

Krishna's words made Gandhari silent. She realised that everything he said was right, but the curse had come out of her lips. Now the curse would come true because Krishna had accepted it. She hoped she would not be alive when her curse came true.

■

The story of Gandhari's curse is found in the Stri Parva of the Mahabharata. Grieving the loss of her sons, Gandhari cursed Krishna, even though she knew their deaths were a result of their own actions.

The destruction of the Yadavas was destined. Krishna's purpose on earth was to reduce the burden of evil, which existed not only among the Kauravas but also among the Pandavas and Yadavas. This is why both sides faced losses.

Gandhari's curse merely echoed what was fated. Even Krishna's death was predestined, as his role ended after the war. Her curse simply became the means for his departure from earth.'

26

Two Curses for Womankind

Sage Dirghatamas was outraged. His wife was casting him out mercilessly. Despite being specially abled, he had done everything to keep her happy—yet she was abandoning him. Dirghatamas' name meant 'Long darkness', symbolising his permanent blindness, a curse from his uncle Brihaspati. He grew up to be a wise man and married Pradweshi, with whom he had many children, including Goutama. Yet, after years of marriage, Pradweshi and her sons decided to exile him. They bound him to wooden planks shaped like a raft and cast him adrift in the Ganga.

'Why do you do this, Pradweshi?' asked the sage. 'I have tried my best to be a good husband to you.'

'You are blind and old. Your presence does not benefit us in any way. Why should we support you? I prefer to live alone without a husband?'

'Vile woman,' said Dirghatamas. 'Your conduct has brought disgrace to women. For your unrighteous conduct, I curse all women. Henceforth, a woman can have only one husband. This shall be the order of the world to be followed by everyone. Even if her husband dies, the woman shall not remarry.'

The angry Pradweshi and her sons pushed Dirghatamas into the water, allowing the river to take him away. Their conduct had led to a rule being imposed through a curse on all womankind. While men could take as many wives as possible, women could not because of what Pradweshi had done.

■

The story of Dirghatamas and his curse is narrated in the *Adi Parva* of the Mahabharata. Bheeshma narrates this story to Satyavati. There was no heir to Hastinapura's throne. Satyavati asked Bheeshma to break his vow of celibacy and marry the widows of the dead king. He then refused and instead suggested that a virtuous Brahmana be brought to impregnate the queens and get heirs from them.

To illustrate his point, Bheeshma narrates the story of Dirghatamas. After Dirghatamas was thrown out in a raft, King Bali saved him. The King had no children. Since Dirghatamas was virtuous, he requested him to impregnate his wife and give him children. Bali's wife then gave birth to sons named Anga, Vanga, Kalinga, Pundra, and Oudhra. All these kings became famous and established kingdoms named after them.

■

Yudhishtira collapsed on the ground, wailing in agony. He could not believe what his mother had told him. The war was over, and Yudhishtira had finished conducting the last rites of all the dead.

That was when Kunti revealed the secret that stunned Yudhishtira and his brothers.

'My son, I have kept a secret from you all these years. Now is the time to reveal it,' said Kunti, shedding tears. Your enemy Karna, who your brother Arjuna killed, was none other than your brother. He was my son, born from my womb.'

Kunti then narrated the story of Karna's birth. Hearing this, Yudhishtira collapsed in shock, unable to bear the burden that this revelation had placed on his shoulder.

'How could you do this, mother?' wailed Yudhishtira. 'Why did you hide this secret for all these years? If you had told me this before the war, I would never have allowed this war to go on.'

'I could not do anything,' cried Kunti, trying to console Yudhishtira. 'I met Karna and requested him to join hands with you, but he refused. He told me that he would spare the lives of four of you in the war but would not spare Arjuna. He said I would still have five sons left after the war, with either he or Arjuna dead after the war.'

'You could have told me all this. I would have done something. By keeping this secret, you are responsible for not just Karna's death but millions of others. Your desire to keep a secret has led to this. I curse all women that henceforth women will never be able to keep a secret in their hearts.'

Uttering this curse, Yudhishtira wept uncontrollably, deciding not to rule over the kingdom and instead retire to the forest.

■

The story of Yudhishtira's curse on womankind is found in the *Shanti Parva* of the Mahabharata. In the *Stri Parva* of the Mahabharata, Kunti reveals the secret of Karna's birth. In the *Shanti Parva*, Yudhishtira asks Narada to tell him about his brother, after which Narada tells the Pandavas the story of Karna and his exploits.

A dejected Yudhishtira cursed womankind, stripping them of their ability to keep secrets. Yudhishtira then refused to rule the kingdom. After a lot of effort, he was persuaded by Bheeshma, Krishna, Narada, Vyasa, and others to change his decision.

The stories of the two curses presented above are significant in terms of the social status of women during those times. Prior to Dirghatamas' curse, women were free and could take husbands and cohabit with any man they wanted. Dirghatamas' curse restricted women from marrying again while men could do so. The rule established by Dirghatamas continued to be a norm in India, with a second marriage for women being frowned upon by society for centuries.

The story revealed the reason for the curse, which was the unreasonable behaviour of one woman for which the entire womankind was cursed. The curse on Kunti is another example of how entire womankind was cursed because of the fault of one woman. There is a belief that women cannot keep secrets, and this curse created this belief.

The Mahabharata is not merely a story, but is Itihasa. It is an account of all that happened and is also an account of the life and social situations in those times.

27
Nachiketa Is Cursed and then gets Boons from Yama

The sage Vajashravasa was busy performing a sacrifice that involved donating cows to the Brahmanas. His son, Nachiketa, noticed that the cows were old, weak, and incapable of giving milk. Worried that his father's actions were sinful rather than virtuous, Nachiketa asked, 'Father, I am young and strong. If you give me away as a donation, you will earn virtues. Who will you give me to?'

The question irritated Nachiketa's father. He was angry that his son indirectly questioned him for donating old cows. The sage who did not have wealth had only these cows to donate. He ignored his son and continued with his work.

Nachiketa was persistent, 'To whom will you give me?'

Vajashravasa lost his temper and shouted in rage, 'I will give you to Yama.'

Determined to honour his father's words, Nachiketa set out for Yama's abode. Despite his father's pleas, the young boy was resolute. He travelled for many days, crossing forests, rivers, and mountains. Finally, he reached the abode of Yama. The guards told him that Yama was not there.

Nachiketa then waited near the door for three days. When Yama returned, he was surprised to see a young Brahmana boy waiting for him. Yama was upset when he learned the boy was waiting for him for three days without food or water.

He took Nachiketa inside and offered him hospitality. He then told the young boy, 'You are my guest and were ill-treated by not being welcomed. To compensate, I offer you a boon for each day you waited for me. Ask anything you want.'

Nachiketa bowed to Yama and said, 'My father has earned demerits because of the act of giving away old and sick cows.

May he earn merits and find peace.'

'I grant this boon. Ask your next boon.'

'I want to learn of the sacred fire sacrifice that would help to earn virtues and reach Heaven.'

'I hereby grant you this knowledge,' said Yama. 'Ask for a third boon.'

'O great Lord. I always wanted to know what happens after death. When a person dies, what happens to him? Please explain the mystery of death.'

Yama thought for a while and said, 'This is too profound knowledge for a young boy like you to know. Ask for anything else. You can ask for riches or palaces. Ask for beautiful women to serve you. Anything you ask will be yours.'

'My Lord, I want nothing material because it will not last. The knowledge of the mystery of death you reveal to me will be immortal, so I seek it.'

Yama was pleased with the young boy's steadfastness. He then explained the secret of life and death.

'When a person dies, it is the outer body that dies. The inner body is the self or the atman. Atma is immortal and never dies. Atma is distinct from the body. The wise person is the one who realises the Atma. One who detaches himself from his body and focuses on the Atma can achieve the supreme consciousness known as Brahman.'

'O Nachiketa, the body is like a chariot. Intelligence is the driver. The five horses in front of the chariot are the five senses. The one sitting inside the chariot is the self, and consciousness is the rein he holds. It is the self that is superior to everything else. The self should control the chariot and not the chariot controlling the self.'

'One's senses can pull a person away from their pursuit.

Just as a charioteer uses the reins to control the horses, one should control the senses and not allow the senses to take control. This is the path to achieving Brahman.'

'One who does not realise this has to repeatedly go through the cycle of birth and death. Each time a person is born, leads a life on earth, dies, and is reborn again. To escape from this cycle and become immortal, one must gain control of the self to achieve Brahman. Mere reading of the scriptures will not help in achieving Brahman.'

'O Nachiketa, the path to realising Brahman is difficult and takes time. One who perseveres will finally achieve this state. This is known as Moksha.'

With these words, Yama revealed the mystery of death to Nachiketa. Filled with wisdom, the young boy returned home to his father, who wept in joy seeing his son back from the abode of death. Nachiketa grew up to be a great sage and ultimately achieved Brahman.

■

The story of Nachiketa is a very famous one. It is not just the story of a wise and brave young boy but is the story of the secret of life and death. A question that intrigues everyone is what happens after death. The story of Nachiketa reveals this mystery with Yama, the God of death himself, being the narrator.

This story is from the Katopanishad, an important Upanishad dealing with philosophy. A different version appears in the Anushasana Parva of the Mahabharata, where Bheeshma, lying on his bed of arrows, narrates it to Yudhishtira. However, this version does not explore the mystery of death. In the Mahabharata's account, Nachiketa's father is called Uddalaki. He sends Nachiketa to fetch firewood from the riverbank. When Nachiketa finds that the firewood has been washed away by the river, he informs his father. Angered by this, Uddalaki curses him, saying, 'You will see Yama.'

Nachiketa then dies and goes to the world of Yama. He is received by Yama, who welcomes the young boy with respect.

Yama then says, 'You are not dead. Your father only said that you should see Yama, and so you are here. Now you must go back, since your father is deeply grieving. I grant you a boon. Ask what you want.'

Nachiketa then asked, 'I wish to see the world that is meant for people who do auspicious deeds.'

Yama then takes Nachiketa and shows him all the worlds. He then tells Nachiketa that the gifting of cows is the most virtuous deed that can be done. He explains the type of cows to be gifted. Nachiketa then returns to his father, who is delighted to see him.

Nachiketa then tells his father about a sacrifice that should be performed that does not require much wealth. This sacrifice would help the person doing this to reach Heaven. The sacrifice would be known as the Nachiketa sacrifice.

28

The Curse of Parvati and the Birth of Skanda

The wedding of Parvati and Shiva came to a joyful end. The Gods were exultant. Shiva, who had lost interest in everything after the death of his wife Sati, was now happy. The Gods were delighted that the Lord of the three worlds had taken a wife, the daughter of Parvata.

They were happier since their union would produce a miracle child. The demon Taraka, who had a boon from Brahma, was harassing gods and humans. Only the child of Shiva could kill Taraka. The Gods had waited many years for this very moment.

However, their happiness was short-lived. The union of Shiva and Parvati had resulted in intense energy being generated. This was unbearable for the Gods. The entire world began to shake, and the Gods feared the intensity of the union would destroy the world.

The Gods went to Shiva with fear in their hearts.

'Tell me what you want?' asked the Lord.

'O' mighty Lord, your energy is supreme. The energy of the mother Shakti is equally powerful. Your union is creating an energy that the world cannot bear. For the sake of the world, I request you to please withdraw your energy.'

Shiva agreed to the request of the Gods and thus saved

the world. He withdrew his energy, but as he withdrew, his seed that had his energy fell to the ground and rolled into the fire, becoming a part of Agni. Unable to bear the impact of this energy, Agni went away and hid in an unknown place.

Parvati could not control her anger at what the Gods had done. 'My husband wanted to have a child with me. This union was needed for the world. But you have stopped my husband, leaving me with no chance of becoming pregnant. I curse all the Gods that you will not have any children henceforth.'

The Gods were shocked by the curse and left from there grieving over the turn of events.

The problem of Taraka increased with the demons he led, increasing the intensity of their attacks on humans and Gods. The Gods went to Brahma to seek a solution.

Brahma told them, 'The son of the Gods alone can kill him. Due to your interference, now none of you can have a child, and neither can Parvati.'

'What do we do now, O Lord? Please give us a solution,' pleaded the Gods.

'There is one solution. When Parvati cursed you, Agni was the only God not present. He is thus immune from the curse. Agni must carry Shiva's energy and use it to produce a child. Only this child can kill Taraka.'

The Gods then went in search of Agni and finally found him. They conveyed the advice of Brahma.

Agni then planted the seed containing Shiva's energy into the river Ganga. The embryo that was formed emitted so much energy that Ganga was shaken.

'I can no longer bear this energy,' cried Ganga. She then released the embryo from her body, and it fell on reeds in the Meru Mountain.

At that time, the celestial beings, the Krittikas, were passing by. Since a single woman could not bear the embryo, Agni split the embryo into six portions for the six Krittikas. The six Krittikas delivered a child at the same time. The six foetuses merged and formed into a boy with six heads and twelve hands.

He was called Kartikeya because he was raised by the Krittikas. He was named Skanda as he was born after the seed fell. Born in secrecy, he was known as Guha. Among the reeds, he became Saravanabhava. With six heads, he was called Shanmukha. As the son of Shiva, he was known as Kumara. Loved by the Brahmanas, he was called Subramanya.

Once he grew up, he was made the general of the forces of the Gods and given the name Senani. Even though he was a young boy, he led the Gods in the battle against the demons. Seated on a peacock and holding an invincible spear, he killed Taraka, ridding the world of his evil.

■

The story of the birth of Kumara is a very famous one in Indian folklore. The great poet Kalidasa composed the epic poem Kumarasambhava, which details the marriage of Parvati and Shiva and the birth of Kumara. There are versions of the story found in both the Ramayana and the Mahabharata.

The story narrated above is found in the *Anushasana Parva* of the Mahabharata. Bheeshma, lying on the bed of arrows, narrates this story to Yudhishtira. This story was originally told by the sage Vasishta to Parashurama. Bheeshma retells this story here. The same story is also narrated in the *Aranyaka Parva*, where the sage Markandeya narrates it to the Pandavas with some changes. Markandeya says that Skanda is the son of Agni and then goes on to say that Agni and Rudra are the same.

The God Skanda is known and worshipped by different names all over India. In the South, he is worshipped as Subramanya and Muruga. While there are different versions of the story of Skanda's birth, the fact remains that Skanda was born as a result of the marriage between Shiva and Parvati. He was the son of Shiva, and his birth helped the Gods kill Taraka.

29

The Curse That Led to Arjuna's Death

After the end of the Kurukshetra war, Yudhishtira was overwhelmed with guilt over the bloodshed and the destruction of the Kauravas. Consumed by grief, he refused to be king. Only after the counsel of Bheeshma, Krishna, Vyasa, and other sages did he finally agree. Vyasa advised him to perform the Ashwamedha sacrifice as atonement for the lives lost in the war. Following this, Arjuna set out with the sacrificial horse across the land. Most kingdoms surrendered peacefully, accepting Yudhishtira's rule, while others challenged Arjuna in battle. During his campaign across Aryavarta, Arjuna arrived in Manipura, ruled by his son, Babruvahana. Arjuna had fathered Babruvahana during his exile, which he undertook after inadvertently breaking the privacy pact by entering Draupadi's chamber while Yudhishtira was present.

During his exile, he was forcibly taken to the world of Nagas by Uloopi. She forced him to marry her and spend a night with her, threatening to kill herself if he didn't agree. Arjuna spent a night with her, after which he proceeded to Manipura.

In Manipura, he saw the princess Chitrangada and fell in love with her. Chitrangada's father was ready to offer

Chitrangada to Arjuna in marriage but with a condition. Chitrangada's son would be the next king of Manipura, and he and his mother would not leave the kingdom to accompany Arjuna to Indraprastha.

Arjuna then married Chitrangada, and a son, Babruvahana, was born to them. After staying for some time, Arjuna returned to Indraprastha. Soon, Babruvahana became the king of Manipura. During the Kurukshetra war, Babruvahana did not participate in the war since he had to remain in Manipura to rule the kingdom as per his grandfather's condition.

When Arjuna reached Manipura, he recollected his days here. When he reached the entrance of the city, his son Babruvahana was waiting for him.

'Father,' said Babruvahana, falling at Arjuna's feet. 'Welcome to Manipura! I am happy to hand over my kingdom to you.'

Arjuna angrily pushed Babruvahana away and said, 'Are you really my son? The son of Arjuna will never submit to another so easily. Fight with me and try to defeat me. If you lose, only then hand over your kingdom.'

Accepting his father's advice, Babruvahana decided to fight a battle with Arjuna and his forces. A fierce archery duel commenced between father and son.

Arjuna was pleasantly surprised to see his son's excellent skills. Even as he appreciated his son's skills, a blazing arrow raced through his defence and struck Arjuna. Gasping for breath, Arjuna collapsed on the battlefield, his life lost.

A shocked Babruvahana and his mother, Chitrangada, wept bitterly. Babruvahana cursed his fate and said that he was responsible for the death of the great Arjuna, whom none could defeat.

Just then, Uloopi arrived. She had befriended Chitrangada, and Babruvahana considered her a foster mother. It was on her bidding that Babruvahana was convinced to fight Arjuna.

'Don't cry, Babruvahana. What has happened was ordained. Arjuna had to die, and it had to be at your hands,' said Uloopi.

'What are you saying, Mother Uloopi? Why should my father have been killed by me?'

'It is because of the curse of the Vasus,' explained Uloopi. 'When your father defeated Bheeshma, the Vasus were enraged and cursed Arjuna to die. My father pleaded with them to revoke the curse. The Vasus agreed but foretold that Arjuna would one day be killed by his own son, thus fulfilling the curse.'

'So, my father's curse is fulfilled?'

'Yes, my child,' smiled Uloopi.

'What is the use if he is dead?'

'I will bring him back to life,' said Uloopi, revealing the Sanjeevani gem of the Nagas. She used its power to revive Arjuna.

Arjuna awoke as if from a deep sleep, surprised to see his two wives and son by his side. On learning what had happened, he was overjoyed. He embraced them warmly and invited them to live with him in Indraprastha.

They agreed, and soon Babruvahana, Chitrangada, and Uloopi joined Arjuna in Indraprastha.

The story of Arjuna being killed by Babruvahana is mentioned in the *Ashwamedhika Parva* of the Mahabharata. While the story of Arjuna's marriage with Chitrangada is narrated in the *Adi Parva*, the *Ashwamedhika Parva* explains the curse of the Vasus and how it was redeemed. What would have ended tragically led to a satisfying ending, with Arjuna being reunited with Babruvahana after losing all his other sons in the war.

Another interesting fact about this story is that this was Arjuna's first-ever defeat in a battle. The only other defeat was by the Kirata, who was none other than Shiva. Arjuna was known to be the greatest warrior in the world and had never been defeated before. He had been pushed back on the defensive before but had not been defeated. This was the first time he faced defeat because of the curse of the Vasus.

30

The Cursed Mongoose and the Sacrifice

Arjuna had returned after the completion of his military campaign. The sacrificial horse had traversed the entire land, ensuring Yudhishtira was lord of the world. Yudhishtira was now ready to carry out the Ashwamedha yajna.

The sacrifice was organised grandly, with kings, sages, and Brahmanas attending from across the country. The Kurukshetra war had resulted in an empty treasury. Vyasa's advice had helped the Pandavas get a treasure trove of wealth from the Himalayas that belonged to King Marutta.

Yudhishtira, known for his charity, gave away riches and cows. He ensured everyone who attended the yajna was fed. The sages praised him, saying that he had earned three times the merit of the sacrifice. They assured him he was now free from the sin of having caused the death of his relatives in the war.

On completion of the yajna, Yudhishtira offered his entire empire to Vyasa, who returned it to him. Three times, the amount of dakshina normally given at sacrifices was distributed. Everyone, including celestial beings, sang praises of Yudhishtira and rejoiced at the success of the sacrifice.

As Yudhishtira relaxed and watched the proceedings, he saw something that surprised him. A mongoose walked towards the altar where the sacrifice was held. He was surprised to see that the mongoose had a body of gold. He was even more surprised that only half of its body was golden.

The mongoose then rolled on the floor, rubbing the side of the body that was not golden on the ground. Everyone assembled for the yajna had noticed the mongoose, and there was now silence. Everyone watched the mongoose roll on the ground for a few minutes.

The mongoose then got up and declared in a human voice, 'O great king, this sacrifice is not equal to the sacrifice done by an ascetic through a tiny amount of barley.'

All the assembled people were taken aback hearing the words of the mongoose.

'How can you say such a thing? The great emperor has given away more in charity than any other king before him. The charity he has done is unparalleled. How can you compare the merits of this great sacrifice to a tiny amount of barley?' questioned a minister.

'I will tell you the story of the ascetic who lived in Kurukshetra with his family. Listen to my story, and then you will understand the meaning of my statement,' said the mongoose.

'There was a terrible famine in the place where the ascetic lived. Food was difficult to come by. With no crops growing, the ascetic would go to the fields and scour for bits of harvested grain. In this way, he would take home a few grains, and his family members would share and eat them.'

'The lack of food had made everyone in the ascetic's home weak, and they looked like skeletons. One day, the ascetic found a handful of barley grains and brought it home. His wife cooked a meal, and the family sat down to eat a meal after many days. Just as they could begin the meal, a guest arrived.'

The ascetic welcomed the guest, who said, 'I am hungry. I have not had food for a long time. I will be happy if you offer me some food.'

The ascetic decided to give his share of the food. Even after eating it, the guest was not satisfied. Then, the wife decided to surrender her share of the food. Even then, the guest's hunger was not satisfied. Then, the ascetic's son and daughter-in-law also gave up their share of the food.

The guest finished the meal and smilingly told them, 'I am Dharma, and I came here to test you. Even though you were starving and on the verge of death, you sacrificed your food for a guest. Your sacrifice is more meritorious than sacrifices done by kings. I am pleased with you. All of you deserve to enter Heaven and live happily.'

A golden chariot appeared, and Yama took the ascetic and his family to Heaven.

'O mighty king,' said the mongoose to Yudhishtira. 'I then rolled on the ground where a few grains of barley had fallen. The half of my body that touched the barley became golden in colour. From that day onwards, I have visited every site of sacrifice and rolled in it, but I could never convert the other side of my body to gold.'

'O, king,' declared the mongoose. 'I came here to see how great your sacrifice was. Even after rolling on this ground, my body did not turn golden. This shows that your sacrifice is not equal to that of the ascetic.'

With these words, the golden mongoose disappeared, leaving the assembled people saddened. Yudhishtira sat quietly in contemplation, wondering how he could have made the sacrifice more meritorious.

■

The story of the half-golden mongoose is narrated in the *Ashwamedhika Parva* of the Mahabharata. This Parva narrates how the Ashwamedha Yajna was conducted. At the end of the Parva, the story of the mongoose is narrated. The story conveys a lesson that a small amount of grain given to a hungry person is more meritorious than a great sacrifice where crores of coins and thousands of cows were given away in charity. The poor ascetic who gave away food even though he was dying was rewarded with Heaven.

The truth behind the story of the mongoose is explained at the end of the *Ashwamedhika Parva*. Vaishampayana, who is narrating the Mahabharata, explains why the mongoose behaved as it did. The mongoose was none other than Krodha or anger, who existed as a celestial being.

Once Krodha offended the great sage Jamadagni and was cursed by his ancestors to become a mongoose. When Krodha pleaded with his ancestors to end the curse, they offered a solution. They told him the curse would end when he spoke ill of dharma. When the mongoose criticised Yudhishtira during the Ashwamedha yajna, he spoke ill of dharma since Yudhishtira was Dharma's son. The moment he did this, he was freed from the curse, regained his original form, and returned to his celestial home.

31

Samba's Curse and the End of the Yadavas

'Let's play a prank on the sages,' said Samba.

His friends laughed uproariously. Samba, the son of Krishna, was known for his reckless behaviour. He did not care about what people thought and did whatever he wanted. Even in the past, he had fallen into trouble many times thanks to his mindless antics.

He had once abducted Lakshmanaa, the daughter of Duryodhana, almost causing a war between Dwaraka and Hastinapura. On another occasion, he had angered the sage Durvasa, who had cursed him to suffer from leprosy. He had to pray to Surya to be cured.

Now, he was inciting his friends to play a prank on the sages Kanva, Narada, and others who were visiting Dwaraka.

'Here is what we will do,' said Samba. 'Let one of us pretend to be pregnant and dress like a pregnant woman. We will then go to the sages and ask them to predict the gender of the unborn child. After the sages make their prediction, we will reveal the prank. It will be great fun.'

His friends cheered him. When it came to the question of who would dress like a woman, they all nominated Samba.

'We are all scared of the sages,' said the friends. 'We cannot pretend to be a woman before them without getting detected. Only you can do it.'

Samba's chest swelled with pride at the compliments from his friends. He went ahead and implemented his foolish prank. His friends dressed him to look exactly like a pregnant woman. They then went to meet the sages.

After bowing to the sages, one friend addressed the sage, 'Respected sages, my friend's wife is pregnant with a child. My friend is keen to know the gender of this child. With your great powers, you can surely see into her womb and let us know. Please do this favour for us.'

The sages looked at Samba, dressed like a woman. Kanva's eyes turned red, and his left eye throbbed. He took deep breaths but could not control his rage.

'You rogues, did you really think you could fool sages like us? You dare to disturb our austerities for this foolish prank?' roared Kanva.

He was not done. Raising a hand with a trembling forefinger pointed at Samba, he uttered the terrible words that sealed the fate of Dwaraka.

'You want to know the sex of the child this so-called woman would deliver? Let me make the prediction. It would be neither male nor female. This man dressed as a woman will deliver a mausala. The mace he delivers will cause the destruction of the Yadava clan.'

The Yadava friends of Samba shook in fear at hearing the words of the sage. They all ran for their lives, Samba following them clumsily, trying to prevent his dress from falling off.

Everyone went to their homes quietly, fearing what would happen. Their fears came true the next day when Samba unexpectedly delivered an iron mace. He was in a state of shock, unable to comprehend how this had happened.

The friends quivered in fear, remembering the words of the sage.

Finally, Samba said, 'Let us tell everything to the King. Let him decide what to do.'

They then went to King Ugrasena. He consulted his ministers and called Krishna and Balarama. After a deep discussion, he summoned his guards and announced his decision. 'Take this mace and pulverise it into powder. Throw the powder into the sea and forget all that happened. This is your last warning, Samba. If you repeat such vile acts, I will throw you out of the kingdom.'

Samba breathed a sigh of relief, believing the worst was over. Alas! Little did he know that the worst was yet to come.

The powder thrown into the sea near Prabhasa grew into Eraka grass. The tip of the mausala could not be crushed and so the guards threw it into the sea. A fish swallowed the tip. A hunter named Jara caught the fish. He went home and cut it open to find the sharp iron object.

Happy with what he found, he fixed the sharp iron tip to an arrow. He decided to use this arrow when he found a worthy target while hunting.

Meanwhile, the Yadavas feuded non-stop. Their behaviour crossed all limits with drunk people fighting each other. Women behaved in the most licentious way. Evil omens were seen regularly, and one day Krishna's Sudarshana Chakra vanished.

After a long discussion, it was decided that the Yadavas would proceed to Prabhasa to spend time praying so their problems would be solved. The drunk Yadavas fought with each other instead of praying. During their fight, they pulled out the Eraka grass that grew on the seashore.

Each blade of the grass pulled out turned into a mace. The Yadavas clutched maces and struck each other. They fought each other until their entire clan was wiped out.

A deeply distressed Krishna went to the forest to mourn in peace. His brother Balarama had gone to a cave to meditate, and he gave up his life. As Krishna rested below a tree, the hunter Jara passed by.

Seeing Krishna's feet with colourful decorations on it, from behind the tree, he thought it to be a deer. He picked up the special arrow and released it. The arrow hit Krishna's toe, ending his life on earth. The vile deed of Samba and the curse of the sages had not just ended the Yadava race but also caused the death of Vaasudeva Krishna.

■

The incident of the Mausala and the sages cursing Samba is mentioned in the *Mausala Parva* of the Mahabharata. This entire volume recounts the terrible incidents in Dwaraka when the Yadava clan was wiped out thanks to their own deeds. Samba, who was believed to be an incarnation of Rudra, had caused the destruction of the Yadava clan.

Subsequently, there was rain, and the sea flooded. The entire city of Dwarka was drowned in the sea. Even today, there is evidence below the Arabian Sea of the ruins of Dwarka. It was a sad end to the legend of Krishna and the Yadavas. The effect of the curses of Gandhari and the sages had made Samba carry out the vile act that ultimately led to the destruction of the Yadavas.

32

How Arjuna Failed Because of Ashtavakra's Curse

The young sage Ashtavakra had immersed his body in water with only his head visible. He prayed and carried out austerities every day. The regular penance he performed had filled him with spiritual power.

One day, as the great sage was engaged in penance, some apsaras passed by. The celestial nymphs were proceeding to Mount Meru to take part in the festivities decked in their best dresses, radiating beauty and grace.

As they passed by the river, they saw Ashtavakra.

'Look at that handsome man,' remarked one of the apsaras. 'Even amidst such intense penance, his face glows with serenity.' 'Indeed,' agreed Tilottama, 'his spiritual power is palpable. His visage is truly captivating.' Another nymph added, 'It is as if the sun itself is reflected in his face, such is his brilliance.'

Even as they praised him, Ashtavakra had completed his rituals. He opened his eyes, looked at the apsaras, and smiled at them.

'I am pleased with your words, celestial women. You can ask me any boon you wish. I will grant them.'

'We do not need any boon. Just seeing you is the biggest boon,' said some of the apsaras.

Smiling at them, the sage waded to the shore of the river and climbed out of it. As the sage came out, the rest of his body was visible. The sage was named Ashtavakra because his body had eight deformities in it. This was the result of a curse by his father, Kahoda.

When he was in his mother's womb, Ashtavakra heard his father reciting the Vedas. The child who had learned the Vedas in his mother's womb detected mistakes made by his father while reciting the Vedas and pointed it out, speaking from his mother's womb. His father was furious and cursed his unborn son with deformities.

Ashtavakra was thus born with deformities in his body. When he came out of the water, these deformities were visible. The entire body was crooked and presented a strange appearance.

The apsaras had seen his attractive face and had expected to see his handsome body as he came out. When they saw his crooked body, they were taken aback. Some of them could not control themselves and started laughing.

Soon, all of them laughed uproariously, amused by the sight of the deformed body of the sage.

'You are celestial beings, yet you mock my deformities. Your behaviour is unbecoming,' he said. 'I had intended to bless you with virtuous husbands, but your actions deserve punishment. You shall indeed marry the best of men, but you will lose them and suffer years of captivity.'

With these words, Ashtavakra turned away, leaving the apsaras regretful and silent.

Uttering this curse, the sage went away even as the apsaras looked on in shock, regretting their words.

All that the sage had said came true. The apsaras had to be reborn on earth. Many of them were abducted by the asura Naraka. Krishna then rescued them. He gave them the status of wives by marrying all of them. They all lived in Dwaraka and had the status of queens.

Thirty-six years after the Kurukshetra war ended, Krishna died as a result of Gandhari's curse. Before he died, he sent a message to Hastinapura, through his charioteer Daruka. As soon as he got the message, Arjuna hurried to Dwaraka. He was stunned to see his beloved friend dead.

Arjuna then finished the last rites of Krishna and other Yadavas. Then, as per Krishna's instructions, he took Krishna's wives and the surviving residents of Dwaraka to Indraprastha, where they would live under the rule of Vajra, Krishna's great-grandson.

The caravan with Krishna's wives moved through the forests, with Arjuna leading the way. Suddenly, there were screams from the women. Bandits were charging at them from the woods. These were the Abhiras, who were known for being thieves. They saw so many women and only one warrior to defend them.

They decided to abduct all the women and take them with them.

Arjuna was in no mood to fight. 'Desist from your vile action. Do not provoke me.'

The thieves laughed at him and continued to loot the caravan, even as many of them grabbed the women.

Arjuna sighed at the fact that he had to fight again. The loss of Krishna had dispirited him, and he had no desire to fight. He picked up the Gandiva and prepared to fight. He was shocked to find that he could not even string his great bow. This had never happened before.

With great difficulty, he strung the bow. But he found it challenging to release arrows. With the help of his guards, he managed to shoot arrows at the Abhiras and managed to kill a few of them. There were thousands of them, and one lone and weakened Arjuna could not do much.

Arjuna decided to use his celestial weapons to destroy the Abhiras. He picked up an arrow and chanted the hymn to invoke the celestial weapon of his choice. He started sweating and his fingers trembled as he realised he had forgotten the hymn. Arjuna could not use any celestial weapons because he did not recollect how to use them.

He then used regular arrows and tried to fight, but it was a one-sided battle. A bigger shock awaited him when he moved his hand to his quiver to take out an arrow. His hand came back empty! There were no arrows in the quiver.

This was the inexhaustible quiver of arrows Varuna had given him. Now it had run out of arrows. Arjuna had lost! For the first time in his illustrious career, Arjuna had failed. He collapsed in his chariot, physically and mentally exhausted, unable to even stand.

Understanding his condition, his charioteer took him away, even as his guards defended him from the bandits. The Abhiras had successfully abducted Krishna's wives, with many of them going with them voluntarily. A broken Arjuna reached Indraprastha with only a handful of Yadavas left. He settled them there and made Vajra their king.

A distraught Arjuna went to meet the sage Vyasa. The sage consoled him, telling him that what had happened was inevitable after the death of Krishna. He then advised Arjuna that his work on earth was done, and it was time to move on.

With a heavy heart, Arjuna returned to Hastinapura to inform his brothers about what had happened. It was time for the Pandavas to leave the world. After Krishna's death and the humiliation he had faced, life had no attraction for Arjuna.

The Vyasa Mahabharata does not have the story about the curse by Ashtavakra that led to Arjuna's failure to defend Krishna's wife. In the Mahabharata's *Mausala Parva*, Vyasa tells Arjuna that the curse of the Brahmanas led to Arjuna losing against the Abhiras. Here, the reference is to the curse of Narada, Kanva, and other sages. It could also be construed as a reference to Ashtavakra's curse.

The story of Ashtavakra being mocked by the apsaras and his curse is narrated in the Vishnu Purana. It is also referred to in a few other Puranas, like the Brahma Purana and the Padma Purana. Even the Devi Bhagawatam has Parvati telling Krishna that his wives would be taken away by robbers due to Ashtavakra's curse.

The Padma Purana provides another reason for this incident. The wives of Krishna see Samba, who was as handsome as Krishna. They then begin to cavort with him. Even though he was the son of their husband, they behaved in a licentious way with him. Seeing this, Krishna cursed them that they would be kidnapped by evil beings as punishment for their sins.

Another version of this incident is available in the Padma Purana. The apsaras playing in the water ask Narada how they could make Narayana their husband. Narada tells them the rites they should carry out to win the hand of Narayana so he could be their husband. At the same time, he condemns them for being selfish and focused on their beauty instead of saluting him. So, he curses them, saying they will be abducted by thieves and end up as courtesans.

THE BOON

A boon is a reward or favour given as a blessing. When it is given by a celestial being, a sage, or someone with special powers, then a boon becomes a benefit and something of value.

You would probably have read many stories about how rakshasas would pray to Brahma for many years and perform severe austerities. Pleased by these austerities, Brahma would grant them a boon. They would then ask for special powers or protection against being killed by Gods.

Blessed by the boon, the rakshasa would create a reign of terror. Thankfully, every rakshasa would leave a loophole in their boon, which would then be used to kill the rakshasa and end his journey of evil.

This is a common theme in many stories in our Puranas. You would have read about Mahishasura becoming a powerful rakshasa by getting a boon that no God could kill him. The Gods then bestow their powers on Parvati, who becomes Goddess Durga and kills the demon.

Similarly, Hiranyakashipu asked for a unique boon. He asked that his death should come neither from a God nor a man, neither inside nor outside, neither in Heaven nor on Earth, neither in the morning nor at night, and without a weapon. Hiranyakashipu thought he was being very smart by asking for this boon, but did not realise that the Gods have a plan for everything.

Vishnu took the leonine form of Narasimha (neither man nor animal) and killed him in the nether world (neither Earth nor Heaven). Hiranyakashipu's killing occurred at the twilight hour (neither morning nor night) and on the threshold of the palace door (neither inside nor outside). Narasimha killed the demon by ripping his stomach open with his nails (not using a weapon).

There are many such stories in our epics of boons asked by demons that are ultimately nullified by Vishnu or another God. There are other stories of boons beneficial to those who asked them or for people at large.

Apart from boons being given by gods and sages, even others could grant boons. Any person who had earned merit by virtue of their good deeds could grant a boon to someone else. The boon they grant would come true thanks to the innate powers of the person granting the boon.

There are many instances of boons in the Ramayana and the Mahabharata. The following pages contain and narrate a few important incidents where boons were granted. In every case, the boons granted had a significant impact on the further course of events. The boons are presented in chronological order of their occurrence.

33

Ravana's Boon

Ravana was deep in meditation, eager to please Lord Brahma. Ravana's penance meant trouble, and the Gods looked on in worry. Asuras like Ravana would get boons from the Gods and misuse them to harass sages and celestial beings.

Ravana's penance was so intense that it caused turmoil in the three worlds. With such an intensive fervour in his prayers, Brahma had no option but to go to him and give him the boons he desired. Not doing so would make him intensify his penance, which would shake up the three worlds.

Brahma appeared before Ravana and told him, 'I am pleased with you, Ravana. Your intense austerities have won over me. Ask any boon you wish. It will be yours.'

'O great Lord, your very presence fills me with energy. I know you will bless me with unlimited strength and valour. What I desire, though, is immortality.'

'You very well know that immortality is available only for the Gods. Ask anything else, and I will grant you the boon.'

'Then give me the option to choose the mode of my death. I should not be killed by Gods, Demons, Pisachas, Gandharvas, Yakshas, Kinnaras, wild animals, or any divine being. This is the boon I ask of you.'

'I grant you the boon you desire,' said Brahma, sprinkling water from his kamandalu on Ravana. Having blessed him, Brahma disappeared.

The blessings from Brahma rejuvenated Ravana, who had become weak after performing austerities for years. Now, virtually no one could kill him. He was the undisputed master of all the worlds.

Laughing loudly, Ravana declared his intentions to the world, 'I am Ravana, the mightiest warrior in the world. I am the invincible leader of all the worlds whom none can kill. I will now show my prowess to the world.'

Indra and the Gods shook in fear, hearing Ravana's roar. They knew Ravana would use his powers to create havoc in the world. They also knew that one day, he would cross all limits, and that would be when he would meet his match.

■

The story of Ravana getting a boon from Brahma is mentioned in the *Bala Kanda* of the Ramayana. The Gods, along with Brahma, met Vishnu and told him how Ravana was torturing the celestials. They told Vishnu that the arrogant Ravana was harassing sages and troubling innocent people.

Vishnu then asked the Gods what strategy he should use to kill Ravana. They then told him to take a human form to eliminate Ravana. The Gods told Vishnu about Ravana's boon from Brahma, offering him protection from gods, demons, and other beings. Ravana, in his arrogance, did not believe any human could kill him.

This loophole in the boon was taken advantage of, and Vishnu was born as a human, Rama. He decided to be born as the son of Dasharatha, who was seeking a son and performing the Putrakameshti yajna to get children.

34

The Boon of Birth

King Dasharatha of Ayodhya was happy. His discussions with the great sages had been fruitful. The king had everything to make him happy. He had a large empire, a great army, three noble and beautiful wives, and a palace worthy of Indra himself.

Unfortunately, the king had no children. Without a son, the great Solar dynasty would have no heir. Dasharatha decided to perform the Ashwamedha yajna or horse sacrifice. This would be followed by the Putrakameshti yajna, a ritual prescribed by the Vedas that would help obtain a son.

Dasharatha had received a communication from the Anga king Romapada. Both the kings had been facing problems. While Dasharatha's problem was that he had no heir, Romapada was facing famine in his kingdom.

The solution in both cases was for Yajnas to please the Gods. It had been decided that Rishyashringa, the son of sage Vibhandaka, must carry out the yajnas. The problem was to bring sage Rishyashringa out of his ashrama.

Romapada had a plan to achieve this. He would send courtesans to Rishyashringa to make him comfortable with the company of women. This was needed since Vibhandaka had brought up Rishyashringa completely isolated from society.

Once Rishyashringa had been convinced to visit Anga,

he would be introduced to Shanta. The idea was to get Shanta married to Rishyashringa. Shanta was the daughter of Romapada. Once Shanta's marriage with Rishyshringa was performed, the sage would carry out yajnas in Anga and Ayodhya.

The communication from Romapada conveyed good news. His plan had worked. Rishyashringa had visited Anga, and the rain god responded by showering rain on the parched kingdom. Shanta was then married to Rishyashringa, who started residing in Anga with his wife.

Hearing this news, Dasharatha proceeded to Anga. He met the sage and pleaded with him, 'O great sage. I do not have an heir to my kingdom. The great race of Ikshavaku will end if I do not get a son. I desire to perform the Putrakameshti yajna to get a son. I request you to preside over the yajna and help me achieve my desire.'

Rishyashringa agreed and left for Ayodhya with Shanta. The city was decorated, and citizens stood in the streets to welcome the sage. Rishyashringa then stayed in Ayodhya with his wife, performing rituals.

When the spring season arrived, Dasharatha met the sage and requested him to conduct the yajna. The sage agreed, and all arrangements were made to perform the yajna on the northern bank of the river Sarayu.

The yajna commenced in the presence of Dasharatha's preceptor, Vasishta. Many kings were invited to attend the sacrifice. Food and clothes were distributed to the citizens, and cows were donated to the Brahmanas.

The horse sacrifice was completed as prescribed by the scriptures. Rishyashringa then carried out the Putrakameshti yajna, in which he was well-versed. When the yajna was completed, a divine being emerged from the fire. In his hands was a golden vessel containing a sweet dish.

The being gave the vessel to Dasharatha and said, 'Give this to your wives, O King. The objective of your yajna to get sons will then be achieved.'

Dasharatha then took the sweet and gave half of it to his first wife and main queen, Kausalya. Of the remaining half, he gave half to his second queen, Sumitra. He then divided the balance into two portions. One he gave to his third wife, Kaikeyi, while the other he gave again to Sumitra.

The queens were thus blessed by the Gods. In due course of time, the queens became pregnant. Kausalya was the first to deliver a child. The son born to Dasharatha and Kausalya would be known as Rama. He was the heir to the throne.

Kaikeyi had a son who was named Bharata. Since Sumitra had two portions of the sweet, she gave birth to twins named Lakshmana and Shatrughna.

Dasharatha was finally happy. He had four sons, with Rama being his heir. He was now assured that the Suryavamsha, started by Ikshavaku, would have a king to take the great lineage forward.

■

The story of the birth of Rama and his brothers is narrated in the *Bala Kanda* of the Ramayana. Dasharatha obtained divine blessings when he carried out the Putrakameshti yajna. The result of the yajna was the birth of his four sons. The story of Rishyashringa and his marriage to Shanta is also narrated here.

The Ramayana says Shanta was Romapada's daughter. But there is a reference to Rishyashringa being Dasharatha's son-in-law. It is believed that Shanta was Dasharathas daughter and was adopted by Romapada.

The Mahabharata has an interesting take on this. In the Adi Parva, there is a statement that Chitraratha's son was Dasharatha, who was also known as Lomapada and his daughter was Shanta. This is stated while narrating about the kings of Anga.

35

The Boon That Led to the Exile

Dasharatha strode into his royal chambers, beaming with pleasure. It was the happiest moment of his life. He was preparing to crown his beloved eldest son, Rama, as the next king.

Every king dreams of having a son who is worthy of ruling his empire. Dasharatha had a son who would be a better king than he was. Rama would be not just the pride of Ayodhya but also the entire Suryavamsha (solar dynasty).

All preparations for Rama's coronation were done. After finishing his meeting with his advisers, Dasharatha went happily to his favourite wife, Kaikeyi's chambers. He wanted to relax and spend a pleasant time with his beloved wife.

He was surprised as he entered the room. It was empty. Kaikeyi would always wait for him, dressed in her best costume, with the smell of incense welcoming him. Today, the room was empty and seemed desolate.

'Where is she?' asked the king turning to the maid who stood near the door.

Bowing low, the maid said, 'The queen is in the anger room.'

Dasharatha groaned. He cursed the person who had invented the anger room. If a queen was offended, she would go to the anger room or chamber of wrath. It was a message to her husband to come and mollify her.

Dasharatha hurried to the anger room, wondering what had gone wrong. He had not done anything to make his wife angry. He charged into the room to find it completely dark. The only light came from the moon outside the window.

He took some time to adjust to the darkness and then saw Kaikeyi lying on the floor, her hair uncombed. He went and sat next to his wife and touched her shoulder gently.

'Wake up, Kaikeyi. Of my three wives, you are my dearest, and you know it very well. I never do anything to hurt you. So why are you angry? Please tell me what makes you angry. I will remove the cause of your anger. Get up, dear.'

Kaikeyi woke up and looked at Dasharatha, her eyes blazing with emotion.

'I am not angry with you husband, but I am hurt.'

'Tell me what makes you feel hurt. I will act immediately. You know how much I love our Rama. In the name of Rama, I swear I will do whatever you say.'

'I am hurt and upset about the fate of my son, Bharata. So I ask you something. Will you promise to give it to me?'

'I have already promised you, my dear. Tell me what you want?' said Dasharatha, caressing Kaikeyi's cheek.

'Do you remember the two boons you gave me many years ago?'

'How can I forget it, Kaikeyi? You came with me to the war. When I was injured, and the wheel of my chariot was broken, it was you who helped me. You repaired the broken wheel and took me away, saving me from death. You took such loving care of me that my health was restored, and I was full of energy ready to continue my battles.'

'You promised me two boons, my king.'

'Yes, but you did not claim the boons then but deferred it for another day.'

'The day has come, my Lord. I want the two boons promised to me today,' said Kaikeyi with a sharpness in her voice that startled Dasharatha.

She got up and clapped. A maid brought a torch, and lit the lamp in the room. Light filled the room, shining on Kaikeyi's face, which glowed with anticipation. The king got up and stood in front of her, eager to know what she desired so much.

'For my first boon, I want my son Bharata to be crowned as the next king.'

'But Kaikeyi, all arrangements are made for Rama to be crowned!'

'That is why I am now asking for my second boon. Rama should go to exile for fourteen years, give up his royal robes and should live the life of an ascetic.'

'No, no, no! How can you ask me this, Kaikeyi? Rama is my life. He is not just Kausalya's son but yours too. You also brought him up and fed him with your hands. How can you ask for such a punishment for your son? I cannot do this, Kaikeyi. Please don't ask for this.'

'O king, you promised to fulfil my desire. You owe me two boons and now is the time I want it. I do not desire any boon other than what I have asked.'

'I know, all this is the work of that wily old woman Manthara,' said Dasharatha, clenching his fists. 'She has poisoned your mind against my Rama.'

Kaikeyi raised her hand imperiously. 'I am not interested in discussing anything else. Just tell me whether you will grant my boons or not.'

Dasharatha pulled his hair and ran around the room, kicking whatever objects he saw and pulling down curtains in impotent rage. Finally, he collapsed, crying loudly, and lost consciousness.

Kaikeyi sprinkled water on his face, and he woke up.

The hard expression in Kaikeyi's eyes worried him. She seemed determined to get her boons.

Dasharatha wailed, 'What wrong has my Rama done? He is just married, and you want to send him to the forest? Rama is the one who will take the race of Ikshavaku forward. He is the pride of Ayodhya and will make me proud by being the greatest King of Raghuvamsha. You know I cannot survive without Rama. How can you be so cruel?'

Kaikeyi did not reply but sat stoically.

'If you feel Bharata is not getting his due, I will rectify it. I will give Bharata whatever he desires. My Rama is such that he will even give up the throne for his brother. You know this very well, and yet you so heartlessly want him to be sent to exile. Don't take the life out of this old man. I beg you, dear wife. Don't ask for this.'

Kaikeyi's eyes had a cruel expression as she glared at the King.

'I have asked for the boons due to me. You have promised it. If you do not give me the boons, you will be guilty of betraying your oath of being a righteous king.'

'The boons you asked are not righteous,' cried Dasharatha, his eyes swollen with tears running down his cheek.

'Righteous or not, give me the boons I desire. If you cannot, then let me know. I will take poison and die. Let posterity know that you are the King who failed to keep his words, and caused his wife's death.'

Dasharatha was shattered. What had promised to be the best time of his life had become the worst. His dream of seeing Rama on the throne would remain unfulfilled. He now had to commit the sin of sending the dutiful Rama into exile.

He wept, pleaded, and even tried to touch Kaikeyi's feet, requesting her to change her mind. Kaikeyi's heart seemed to have turned to stone. She remained unmoved, insisting that her two boons be granted.

Everything was over for Dasharatha. His life was in ruins. He would have to send Rama to exile, which was like tearing his heart out. Dasharatha knew the next few days would be the most painful in his life. He prayed for death to take him away instead of having to commit this sin.

All of Dasharatha's fears came true. Left with no option, he had to send Rama to exile. He stood on his balcony, shedding tears as he watched Rama leave the palace dressed in barks, along with his young wife Sita and his brother Lakshmana.

A man without his heart cannot live, and neither did Dasharatha. After suffering for a few painful days, Dasharatha died a heartbroken man without seeing his son before his death.

■

The story of Dasharatha's boons to Kaikeyi appears in the *Ayodhya Kanda* of the Ramayana. It is a significant episode as it changes the flow of events, with Rama going into exile. Dasharatha's act of giving boons to his wife and allowing her to defer them proved to be disastrous. He suffered the ignominy of exiling his beloved son to the forest while he pinned away to death.

The turn of events is significant, because it is in the forest that Ravana abducts Sita. Rama then goes in search of his wife and kills Ravana, thus ending his reign of evil. The story is an example of how boons granted could lead to a disaster. Lord Shiva granted a boon, and Bhasmasura tried to kill Shiva with his own boon. Vishnu then came in the form of Mohini and saved Shiva.

Unfortunately for Dasharatha, no one was there to save him. The boons he gave finally led to his death. The person who asked for the boons also did not benefit. Her son did not become king. Kaikeyi was reviled by all, including her own son.

Ultimately, it was Rama who asked Bharata to forgive Kaikeyi. This is a story of boons that caused chaos all around. It is also a reiteration of the curse by Shravana Kumara's parents that ensured Dasharatha would die after being separated from his son.

36

The Boon of Mighty Weapons

Vishwamitra was happy seeing Rama's valour. He had made the right decision by going to Ayodhya and asking King Dasharatha to send Rama and Lakshmana with him. The two princes had displayed their valour and rid the forests of the demons that stayed there and harassed sages and common folk.

The most terrible Tataka, who harassed sages and killed innocent people was dead. Rama had easily killed the terrible demoness using his unparalleled skills in archery.

Vishwamitra told Rama, 'Prince of Ayodhya, I am pleased with your valour. When I came to your father, he was apprehensive. He told me you were young boys and was scared to send you with me. In fact, he wanted to come himself. I am happy that I convinced him to send you. Now you have proved that you are the greatest warrior in this world.'

Rama bowed to the sage and said, 'It is the blessings of elders that have made me skilled in the art of archery.'

'Rama, you deserve to have all the powers to make you the greatest archer in all the three worlds. Your dedication has impressed me. You deserve to have the celestial weapons of the Gods. With these weapons, you can defeat anyone in the world. Your fame will be unsurpassed, and you will be known as the warrior king.'

With these words, Vishwamitra gave the most precious boon to Rama—the boon of celestial weapons that would make him an all-powerful warrior, one whom none could defeat.

'I give you the great discus of time and virtue you can use to punish evil. I grant you the Vajra, the thunderbolt of Indra. I give you the trident of Shiva, along with the almighty Brahmashira missile and the Brahmastra.'

The great sage recited the hymns that invoked the celestial weapons, as he gave them as boons to Rama.

'I give you the maces Modaki and Shikhari. I grant you the nooses of Yama and Varuna, as well as the missile of Varuna. This is the Pinaka missile of Shiva and the Narayanastra of Vishnu. I give you the Shushka missile that dries up and the Aardra that drenches. Here is the missile of Agni with the blower missile of Vayu.'

Continuing to chant hymns, Vishwamitra granted more boons. 'This is the horse-head missile of Vishnu and the heron-head missile of Shiva. I give you the rods Kankalam, Kapalam, and Kankanam that the demons have so you can crush them. Here is the missile Vaidhyadhara and the sword Nandana.'

Rama bowed before the great sage, accepting the weapons belonging to the Gods.

Vishwamitra continued with his spree of boons, 'This is the Mohana missile of the Gandharvas that renders unconscious and the Praswapana that causes sleep. The Prashamana that pacifies enemies and the Maanava weapon that controls the wild are yours. The Pishacha weapon of the demons and the Teja Prabha of Surya are yours. Varshana the rainer, Shoshana the drainer, Santapana the humidifier, Vilapana the inducer of tears; Tamasa, Saumana, Samvarta, Mausala, Satya, Maya, Shishira, and the Sudaamna of Twashtra are now yours.'

The array of weapons Vishwamitra gave made Rama the most powerful being on earth. Even the celestials did not have so many weapons with them. This was a rare instance where a human possessed the most powerful weapons in the world. With humility, Rama accepted the weapons from Vishwamitra and learned the hymns to invoke them.

Having accepted the weapons and the blessings of Vishwamitra, Rama, along with his brother, continued his journey to the ashrama of the sage.

Of all the boons found in the epics, the boons given by Vishwamitra to Rama are possibly the most powerful boons. These boons gave Rama the ability to use celestial weapons belonging to the Gods. With these weapons, Rama now could take on anyone in the world. He could now fight with any of the demons in the world, including Ravana.

■

The story of Vishwamitra granting boons to Rama is found in the *Bala Kanda* of the Ramayana. Prince Rama had to become the warrior prince who could uphold dharma and rid Earth of evil. This was the reason for which Rama had taken birth on earth. To make this a reality, Vishwamitra gave these mighty weapons to Rama.

Rama was none other than Vishnu Himself, but neither did he realise that he was Vishnu nor did he possess the weapons that belonged to Vishnu. He had to be given the weapons so he could rid the earth of its burden. Interestingly, Krishna knew he was God and possessed the powers and weapons Vishnu's incarnation needed to have. Both of them had come to earth to reduce the burden of evil on earth, and they finally achieved their goals.

37

The Boon That Unseated a King

The great sacrifice was in progress. Hundreds of kings were present, along with celestials, to watch the sacrifice. Sages narrated hymns under the supervision of the preceptor, Shukra. Seated in front of the sacrificial fire was Emperor Bali.

The celestials seated in the venue looked on enviously at Bali. There was no doubt that the grandson of Prahlada was a virtuous man. Known for his benevolent rule and his adherence to dharma, Bali donated gold coins and cows during the sacrifice to the deserving. Tens and thousands of people were fed, and they praised Bali Chakravarti.

Bali's might had led him to become the Lord of not just one world but all the worlds. With his might, he had subdued Indra and become the Emperor of the Universe. While his subjects were happy with him, the Gods were worried, because an Asura king had dethroned them.

Already, Bali's arrogance was leading to the Gods being humiliated. There would be a time when they would be thrown out of the celestial world with asuras reigning over the world. This could not be allowed, and the Gods had appealed to the great Lord Vishnu to protect them. They eagerly awaited his arrival.

The sacrifice was coming to a close. Soon, it was time to honour the sages and the Brahmanas. Even as Bali was carrying out his work, there were the sounds of murmuring throughout the hall. Bali looked up to find out the reason for the noise.

Everyone looked on as a dwarf strode into the hall. Tiny in appearance, resembling a small boy, the person who walked into the sacrificial venue was a man. The Vamana, with stunted growth, took long strides with a smile on his face.

An unexplainable radiance emerged from him, making him the centre of attraction. Clearly, the Vamana was a very virtuous ascetic. Bali stood up and welcomed the diminutive ascetic with folded hands.

'I am blessed with your presence, O enlightened one. Permit me to honour you,' said Bali, ushering Vamana into the chair kept for honouring the sages. Bali washed Vamana's feet, offered flowers, and sought his blessings.

'O great Chakravarti,' said Vamana. 'I have heard a lot about your charitable nature. It is said that you never deny charity to anyone.'

'You have heard right,' said Bali with a smile on his face. 'Ask whatever you want, and I will give it to you.'

'Are you sure about this?' asked Vamana. 'Can you give anything I ask and not deny my wish later?'

'Bali has never gone back on his word. Ask the boon you desire. I will give it to you, whatever it is and whatever it costs. This is my word.'

Acharya Shukra whispered to the king, 'Be careful, Bali. This dwarf is not an ordinary man. This is a ploy by the Gods. Do not offer him a boon.'

Turning to the guru of the Asuras, Bali said, 'I do not care who he is. I have promised him a boon and will give it come what way. Do not ask me to give up my *dharma*.'

The furious Shukra said, 'Your arrogance has brought you

to this stage, that you disregard your preceptor's suggestions. I will no longer stay in your kingdom. You will remember how true my words were very soon.' With these words, Shukra left the kingdom of Bali.

Bali turned to Vamana and said, 'I have given you, my promise. Tell me what you seek.'

'All I want is some land I can cover in three steps.'

The entire hall burst out laughing when they heard what Vamana sought.

Bali's minister mocked Vamana, 'Your three steps won't even cover the entrance to a hut. What will you do with so little land? My Chakravarti is benevolent and will give you anything. Don't miss this chance by asking something as meaningless as this.'

Vamana smiled and addressed Bali, 'Will you grant my boon?'

'I have already given you my word. Go ahead and place three steps. The space covered by the three steps will be yours.'

There were loud gasps in the hall as the dwarf turned large. The gasps turned to shouts of panic, with people fleeing as the dwarf grew in size. Soon, Vamana was as high as the sky. He lifted his foot, raised it in the air and placed it on the Heavens. He lifted the other foot and placed it on earth.

'I have placed two steps, Bali. I don't see any place to place the third step. Tell me, where shall I place the third step?' questioned the booming voice of Vamana.

'Place it on my head, my Lord,' said Bali, kneeling before the massive Vamana.

Vamana placed his foot on Bali's head and pushed him into the netherworlds. The Gods cheered seeing Bali being banished to the underworld. Bali's subjects and ministers wailed at the loss of their emperor who had been exiled.

There was a searing flash of light, and in place of Vamana stood Vishnu.

'I am pleased with you, Bali. You offered me your head even though you knew what I would do. You have proved to be a great follower of *dharma*. I grant you the boon of immortality. You shall never face death. In the eras to follow, you will gain the position of Indra.'

With these words, Vishnu disappeared as Bali left Earth and moved to the nether worlds.

■

The story of Vamana and Bali is a part of the Ramayana and appears in the *Bala Kanda*. The sage Vishwamitra narrates the story to Rama. When Vishwamitra takes Rama and Lakshmana with him to fight demons, he narrated many tales to them. As they entered the forest, he showed them the place where Vamana lived. He then went on to narrate the story of Vamana and Bali.

Bali is considered a great king, who unfortunately, suffered from the arrogance that most asuras had. For this, he was sent into exile and dethroned. However, Vishnu blessed him with immortality and people remember the greatness of Bali even today. In many places in India, Bali Padyami or Bali Pratipada is celebrated during Deepavali to remember the great king.

There is a folktale in Kerala, according to which Bali asked permission to return to earth for one day every year to see his subjects. Vishnu granted this boon. Every year, Keralites celebrate the return of Bali as Onam. The harvest festival commemorates the greatness of Bali.

38

The Boon That Purified Souls

The white horse roamed around the entire country. Following the horse were the sons of King Sagara. Whenever the horse went through a kingdom, the king had two options. One was to accept the rule of King Sagara and offer tributes. The other was to seize the horse.

If the second option were exercised, then the sons of King Sagara would engage in war with the kingdom. Considering the strength of the army of Ayodhya, the victory of King Sagara's troops was a foregone conclusion. Most kingdoms preferred to accept the rule of King Sagara.

This was how the Ashwamedha yajna worked. When the horse finished its sojourn, Sagara would be the ruler of the entire earth once the sacrifice was complete. Indra was upset and worried that once Sagara became the king of the earth, he would turn his attention to Indra's throne.

Indra arrived on earth at night when everyone was asleep. He quietly took away the sacrificial horse and hid it in the hermitage of sage Kapila. Indra's intention was to create trouble, and it worked.

The next day, the sons of Sagara saw the horse was missing. They went on a rampage, searching everywhere for it. They did not find it anywhere and dug into the earth to reach the netherworld to search for the horse.

When they reached the northeast, they arrived at the ashrama of sage Kapila.

'Look, the horse is there,' shouted one prince.

'The vile sage has stolen our horse. Let us teach him a lesson,' screamed another of the princes.

Brandishing their weapons, the princes charged towards the sage, who was deep in meditation.

Just as they were about to attack the sage, he opened his eyes. Kapila was so powerful that the moment he opened his eyes, flames emitted from it. Angry at his meditation being disturbed, the sage burnt the sons of King Sagara, turning them into ashes.

Sagara, meanwhile, awaited the arrival of his sons with the horse. When they did not turn up, he summoned his grandson, Anshuman.

'O Anshuman, your uncles, and the sacrificial horse are missing. Without the horse, my sacrifice will be incomplete. Go find the horse and your uncles.'

Anshuman then set out to find the horse. After scouring the entire earth, he finally arrived at sage Kapila's ashrama, where he spotted the horse. He also saw the pile of ashes and was shocked.

He then noticed a huge eagle perched upon a tree. Anshuman recognised it to be Garuda, the vehicle of Lord Vishnu.

Garuda then explained all that had happened.

'O prince, the sons of King Sagara were arrogant, vile, and evil. They got their well-deserved punishment for daring to accuse Sage Kapila of stealing the horse. The sage is none other than a form of Lord Vishnu. Now, your uncles have been reduced to ashes.'

Anshuman wept on seeing the ashes of his uncle. He decided to perform the last rites but could not find water anywhere. He knew the souls of his uncles would not reach Heaven until their last rites were performed.

He turned to Garuda and sought his help.

'In the past, when the Gods and the demons warred, the demons had hidden in the ocean,' said Garuda. 'The Gods then went to the sage Agastya and sought his help. He drank all the water from the ocean, allowing the Gods to destroy the demons. When they asked him to restore the water, he said it was not possible to do so because he had digested it. There is no water now to purify the souls of your uncle. You need to bring the holy river Ganga to Earth. That is the only way to achieve your goal.'

With these words, Garuda flew away. Anshuman took

the horse and went back. Sagara was then determined to bring Ganga to Earth so his sons would get redemption. He failed to do so in his lifetime. Anshuman also tried, but was unsuccessful.

Anshuman's son Dileepa then tried to bring Ganga to earth but could not succeed and died, having failed to complete this mission. Dileepa's son Bhagiratha was determined to complete the mission that his father and grandfather could not. Handing over the kingdom to his wise ministers, he went to the Himalayas to pray.

He spent countless years in meditation, determined to please Lord Brahma. Finally, pleased with his devotion, Brahma appeared before him.

'Bhagiratha, I am pleased with your penance. Ask any boon you wish.'

'O Lord, I want the souls of my ancestors to be purified. For this, the river Ganga, who resides in Heaven, needs to come to earth. I seek your blessings for this to happen.'

Brahma said, 'I will ensure that the daughter of Himavan, Ganga, comes to earth. The descent of Ganga from Heaven to earth will be so powerful that it will cause massive floods and destroy everything. Her forceful descent must be controlled, and only Lord Shiva can do that.'

Bhagiratha then performed penance to please Lord Shiva. When Shiva appeared, Bhagiratha pleaded with him to stop the force of Ganga.

Shiva said, 'I will use my head to stop the force of Ganga. She will then flow in a normal course, and your mission will be successful.'

Ganga then descended to earth. Shiva opened his hair and stopped Ganga, trapping her in his head. With the force reduced, the river flowed smoothly, forming the Bindu Lake. From there, Ganga followed Bhagiratha, creating many tributaries. Finally, Ganga reached the underworld, where the ashes of Sagara's son awaited redemption.

The moment the waters of the Ganga touched the ashes, the souls of Sagara's sons were liberated. The pleased Bhagiratha thanked Ganga who then flowed towards the ocean, filling it with water.

Bhagiratha had thus helped his ancestors reach Heaven. In the process, he ensured the river Ganga was brought to earth.

■

The descent of Ganga is narrated in the *Bala Kanda* of the Ramayana. Sage Vishwamitra told Rama and Lakshmana that performing rituals in Ganga's waters purifies sins, and merely hearing the tale of her descent grants spiritual cleansing.

Ganga is also referred to as Bhagirathi, thanks to the effort of Bhagiratha in bringing Ganga to earth. The effort of Bhagiratha is recognised by using the term '*Bhagiratha prayatna*' to refer to any task that is difficult to achieve and requires dedication. This term is equivalent to 'Herculean effort' from Greek mythology.

Revered as Papanashini, Ganga is believed to absolve sins of all who come into contact with her. The story is also recounted by Sage Lomasha to the Pandavas in the *Aranyaka Parva* of the Mahabharata.

The story explains why the river Ganga is given so much importance in Indian culture. The river and its tributaries are worshipped. People bath in these waters, hoping their sins would be washed away. The river also sustains life by offering a water source for millions of people who live near the river.

39

The Boon That Made Hanuman Almighty

The little monkey looked up at the sky, and saw a red ball. He was feeling hungry and wanted food. He could not see his mother anywhere, and he was not ready to wait for food.

He did not know what the red ball was, but it looked like the delicious fruit that his mother would serve him. Standing up, he reached out to the ball with his hands but could not reach it because it was high in the sky.

Bending down, the son of Anjana leapt into the air. The leap was so powerful that it took him all the way to the red ball, which was the Sun. The Sun blazed in fury and released heat waves to stop the monkey.

The monkey was least perturbed by the heat and kept moving in the air, trying to grab the huge Sun. Scared by this, the Sun shot up in the air. The entire atmosphere in the world changed because of the Sun moving away.

Coming to know of this, Indra set out on his elephant, Airavata, to find out what was happening. Seeing the monkey chase the Sun, Indra was furious. Racing towards the monkey, Indra shouted, 'Stop monkey, what are you doing? Stop at once.'

Seeing Indra, the monkey let out a shriek of joy. He had seen the white elephant and wanted to play with it. The monkey leapt towards Airavata, intending to grab the elephant. The elephant was startled and moved back, causing Indra to totter.

The furious Indra took out his mighty Vajra and hurled it at the monkey. Any living being hit by the Vajra would face instant death. The thunderbolt raced through the air, creating an ear-splitting noise even as the sky became dark and streaks of lightning appeared.

The thunderbolt hit the monkey child on his face. Shrieking in pain, the monkey fell to the ground. Even as the monkey was about to fall to the ground, someone picked him up. It was his father, Vayu, the wind god. Vayu was wild with anger at seeing how Indra had hit his son.

He decided to teach Indra a lesson. Taking his unconscious son in his arms, he hid in a cave. The absence of the wind caused chaos in all the worlds as people struggled to breathe. Indra then requested Brahma to help them. Led by Brahma, Indra accompanied by the other Gods went to the cave.

'Come out, Vayu,' said Indra. 'If you stay here, millions will die.'

'You hurt my child,' said Vayu, coming out and showing his son, whose face was swollen with the impact of the thunderbolt. Other than that, there were no other injuries.

'I am sorry, but I had no option but to do this, when I saw your son attack me,' said Indra, trying to defend himself.

'Look at my son now, his face is all swollen, and he will grow up with a swollen face.'

Brahma smiled at Vayu and said, 'Your son's red & swollen face will be how the entire world identifies him. He will be known as Hanuman, and will be one of the mightiest beings on Earth. I bless him with the boon that no missile or weapon can ever harm him.'

Indra then told Vayu, 'Your son will become very famous. I give him a boon that he will live eternally and be a *Chiranjeevi* who will decide when he wants to leave the Earth. He will have the power to change his form as and how he pleases.'

Eager to appease Vayu, all the Gods showered boons on Hanuman.

Surya told Vayu, 'Your son will be as effulgent as I am and will shine in the world.'

Agni told him, 'Fire can never harm your son.'

Varuna gave the boon that water could never harm Hanuman.

Yama then gave the boon that Hanuman could not be caught by any noose.

Kubera blessed him, saying, 'He will be all-powerful and never get tired in battle.'

'Are you happy now, Vayu?' asked Brahma. 'Your son will become famous and be known as Maruti since you are Marut. He will be called Anjaneya after his mother, Anjana. He will have the ability to move faster than the mind and will be known as Manojava.'

Vayu was pleased with the various boons his son got. He bowed before Brahma, and all the Gods blessed Hanuman, who was now awake and cheerful. Vayu then took him back to his mother and left him with her, where he would grow to become a mighty member of the Vanara clan.

■

The story of Hanuman getting a boon from Lord Brahma is mentioned in the *Kishkinda Kanda* of the Ramayana. When the monkeys searching for Sita are contemplating how to cross the ocean to go to Lanka, the bear Jambavan reminds Hanuman of his powers. He reminds him of the story of his birth and how he gained powers.

The story of Hanuman leaping towards the sun is one of the most famous tales in Indian folklore, and is the basis to explain Hanuman's superpowers. The powers remain hidden until the time comes when he has to use them to go to

Lanka. When he reaches Lanka, he demonstrates his might. The Shiva Purana says that Hanuman is an incarnation of Shiva, which is why all the Gods bless him with boons.

At the end of the Ramayana, when Rama leaves his human form and returns to the world of Vishnu, Hanuman seeks his permission to remain on Earth. He tells Rama that he will live on to spread the name of Rama. There is another story in which Rama sends Hanuman on an errand to retrieve his ring, which had fallen below the earth. Rama did this so Hanuman would not be present to grieve, when the time came for Rama to leave Earth.

While the boon of Brahma gave Hanuman supernatural powers, he never misused it. Neither did he display arrogance. He used his powers only to take on the rakshasas. Hanuman is known not only for his powers but also for being a faithful devotee of Rama. Hanuman makes an appearance even in the Mahabharata where he meets Bheema and promises to sit on Arjuna's flag to roar and create terror in the minds of the opponents of the Pandavas.

40

The Pushpaka Vimana

Kubera sat deep in meditation, praying to the creator, Lord Brahma. The Lord of Lanka, King of the Yakshas, and the master of riches had everything in the world. Yet he prayed to Brahma for a boon.

Soon, the creator appeared before him, pleased with his austerities.

'Kubera, I am pleased with your devotion. I have come before you to bless you. Ask whatever boon you wish. I will grant it to you.'

Kubera bowed before the Lord and said, 'O Lord, with your blessings, I have everything I need in the world. However, I covet something, and it belongs to you. I will be blessed if you give it to me.'

'Ask what you want. I will not deny it to you,' smiled Brahma.

'Then please give me the Pushpaka Vimana,' pleaded Kubera, his hands folded before the Lord.

'The aerial vehicle built for me by Vishwakarma? You want that as a boon?'

'Yes, my Lord. I have everything in the world. You are the creator, and can travel anywhere at the speed of thought. I want a vehicle that I can use to travel and reach my destination quickly. I desire your Pushpaka Vimana to help me travel through the world to discharge my responsibilities.'

'Take it, Kubera,' said Brahma. 'The aerial vehicle will take you anywhere in the world. It will work on your command. The owner of this vehicle has to just think of the destination, and it will take him there. You can control the vehicle using your mind.'

Blessing Kubera, Brahma vanished. In his place stood the Pushpaka Vimana. The beautiful golden vehicle was massive. It had a throne fit for a king. Kubera got into the vehicle and sat on the throne. There was space inside for his ministers, advisers, guards, wives, and anyone else he wished to accommodate.

The vehicle was rectangular and had a dome on the top to offer protection from the rain and sun. The dome was decorated with gems of various kinds that shone in the sun's light. On the sides of the vehicle were etched the images of divine beings.

Seated on the throne, Kubera thought of Lanka. The vehicle immediately took off in the air. Gliding smoothly, it moved towards Lanka, taking Kubera back to his kingdom. Kubera wanted to see the mountains, and the vehicle rose high in the air. Indeed, it could be controlled by thought.

Kubera was happy with his acquisition. He could now travel from Lanka to the land of Yakshas easily.

Alas! Kubera's happiness did not last long. His half-brother Ravana was gaining in strength. Though they shared the same father, Kubera and Ravana were diametrically opposite in nature. Kubera was good-natured, while Ravana had a streak of evil in him.

His boons from Brahma gave Ravana immense strength. He then attacked his own brother. Charging into Lanka with his forces, Ravana defeated Kubera's army, causing mayhem in Lanka. One of the first things Ravana did on reaching Lanka was to seize the Pushpaka Vimana.

Deprived of his vehicle and kingdom, Kubera fled from Lanka. He retired to the mountains of Alakapuri, from where he continued to rule over the Yakshas, having lost much of his wealth to Ravana.

■

The description of the Pushpaka Vimana is found in the *Sundara Kanda* of the Ramayana. When Hanuman lands in Lanka, he sees this aerial vehicle. The vehicle is described previously, when Ravana uses it to abduct Sita. The Ramayana mentions how Ravana seized the vehicle from his brother Kubera when he took control of Lanka.

The architect of the Gods, Vishwakarma, built the aerial vehicle for Brahma, who gave it as a boon to Kubera. Ravana seized the vehicle from his brother. After the death of Ravana, Rama uses the Pushpaka Vimana to return from Lanka to Ayodhya. The Ramayana mentions how he could cover the distance within a day. Finally, the Vimana goes back to its original owner, Kubera.

The Vimana is described as being like a mountain with many peaks on it. This description seems to indicate the Pushpaka Vimana was not a small vehicle but a huge one. It is mentioned that the vimana was one yojana long and one yojana wide (approx. area of 58 square miles).

The Vimana was not just a vehicle, but also a palace. Hanuman enters the vimana and sees that it is Ravana's palace. It was so beautiful that Hanuman felt he had entered Heaven. The vimana and palace were where Ravana stayed with Mandodari and his other wives.

41

Indra's Boon to Rama

Ravana was dead. The war between the forces of good and evil was over. Rama and his troop of Vanaras had won the war for the liberation of Sita. After the war was over, a miraculous sight was witnessed.

A golden chariot descended from the sky. It was Indra's chariot, the same chariot that was given to Rama to use in his fight against Ravana. The chariot now had Indra in it. With Indra was a familiar figure, the sight of whom filled Rama's heart with joy.

It was his father, Dasharatha. Indra had brought Dasharatha's ethereal form to earth to enable the father and son to meet. Rama, who had not been able to see his father's body for one last time, was overjoyed to see Dasharatha again. Father and son had an emotional reunion as Indra watched smilingly.

Ravana was a threat even to the world of gods, and Indra has been troubled in the past by Ravana. Ravana's son Meghnad had defeated him, after which Meghnad got the title Indrajit. Indra was keen to see the end of Ravana and was delighted that Rama had got rid of Ravana.

Once Rama had finished spending time with Dasharatha, they bid goodbye as Dasharatha's soul returned to Heaven.

Indra bowed to Rama and said, 'O Lord Rama, you have reduced the burden of evil on earth by killing Ravana. Ask for a boon, O great king. I will grant you whatever you ask for.'

Hearing Indra's words, Rama thought for some time. He then asked the boon.

'O Lord of the celestials. Many tens and thousands of Vanaras have died in the war for me. Death has cruelly separated them from their wives and children. If you wish to grant me a boon, I pray you bring the dead Vanaras back to life and fill them with energy. Let there be abundant water, fruits, roots, and flowers wherever they live. This is the boon I ask of you.'

Indra replied, 'O great Rama, no one has asked for the boon of restoring the dead to life. This has not been done before, but for your sake, I will do it. All the monkeys who were dead will come back to life, restored to health, and filled with energy. As per your wishes, their land will be filled with rivers and trees that bear flowers, fruits, and roots at all times.'

Indra's boon led to all the dead monkeys waking up as though they had gone to a long sleep. The monkeys whose heads were severed had their heads joined again. Monkeys whose limbs were cut had their limbs restored. All the dead Vanaras were alive once again, hale, healthy, and full of vigour.

Indra then told Rama, 'Send back the monkeys to their abode. Your brother Bharata awaits you and is spending all his time in sorrow after being separated from you. Seeing you will fill him with happiness. O Rama, go back to Ayodhya and rule the kingdom. Your mothers and your citizens await you.'

With these words, Indra mounted his chariot and left for his abode.

The happy Rama and Lakshmana then made arrangements to return to Ayodhya.

■

The story of Indra's boon to Rama is narrated in the *Yuddha Kanda* of the Ramayana. After the war between Rama and Ravana, Indra grants a boon that restores the lives of all dead Vanaras. Rama then returns to Ayodhya to rule over the kingdom and establish a reign of prosperity known as Rama Rajya.

42

The Story of the Mighty Kartavirya

Yayati's son Yadu formed his own kingdom after his father threw him out of his kingdom for failing to surrender his youth to his father. In Yadu's race was born a mighty king known as Arjuna. His father was Kritavarya, and hence he was known as Kartavirya Arjuna.

Desirous of being a mighty and successful king, Kartavirya decided to pray to Lord Datta, the son of the Trimurthis.

The King of Mahishmati performed severe penance for many years. Finally pleased with his devotion, Datta appeared before him, showing his divine form.

'Ask any boon you wish, Arjuna. I am pleased with your devotion,' said Datta. 'In fact, I am so happy that I have decided to give you four boons. Think carefully and ask the boons that will help you.'

Kartavirya was ecstatic at the prospect of getting four boons.

He bowed to Lord Datta and asked for his boons.

'Great Lord, for my first boon, I want to be immensely powerful with the strength of a thousand arms. With this power, I do not want to go on the path of *adharma*. In case I stray, I request that a person who is virtuous stop and correct me. For the third boon, I want to conquer the entire earth without straying from the path of *dharma*. For my final boon, I should have the power to kill all my enemies, and only someone who is superior to me in all ways should slay me.'

Datta smiled and raised his hand in blessings, 'I grant you all your boons. May you be successful.'

A happy Kartavirya then returned to his kingdom and set out to conquer the world. Kingdom after kingdom fell before him, unable to stand up to his might. Having conquered the world, Kartavirya performed sacrifices and gave away charity to thousands of people.

Everyone praised the king for his virtuous behaviour. The mighty king ruled over the Earth, respected by his subjects and feared by his enemies. He had a hundred sons, but lost many of them in the battles that were fought. In the end, he was left with only five sons.

His sons had become arrogant with power. Kartavirya

had also become arrogant that he had no match in the world. One day, he ransacked the hermitage of Apava, the son of Varuna.

The furious Apava told Kartavirya, 'You arrogant man. You must be taught a lesson. Rama, the son of Jamadagni, will cut off all your arms and kill you. Your arrogance will then get the punishment it deserves.'

As per Datta's boon, Kartavirya had been corrected when he strayed from the path of dharma. He then continued to rule wisely by following *dharma*. However, his sons continued to stray to the path of *adharma*. As a result, other Kshatriyas across the earth also began to follow *adharma*.

One day, the sons of Kartavirya came across the ashrama of sage Jamadagni and entered it when he and his son were not there. They insulted Jamadagni's wife Renuka, and took away the calf of their beloved cow that they worshipped.

Rama, the son of Jamadagni, was known as Parashurama because of the gift of the Parashu or axe that he had won from Lord Shiva. When he learned about the vile act of Kartavirya's sons, he angrily stormed the palace of Kartavirya.

There, Rama saw the calf, separated from its mother, wailing piteously. His blood boiled in fury, and he went to take away the calf. Seeing him, Kartavirya came out and challenged him.

The mighty Rama was none other than the incarnation of Lord Vishnu, who had come to earth to reduce the burden of evil by getting rid of the arrogant and vile Kshatriyas.

Rama picked up his mighty axe and charged at Kartavirya. The king laughed at seeing Rama. Picking up weapons in each of his arms, he attacked Rama. Swinging his mighty axe, Rama hacked off all the hands of Kartavirya. Wild with anger, Rama struck Kartavirya on his head, killing him.

When Kartavirya's sons came to know about what happened, they went to the ashrama of Jamadagni in search of Rama. They did not find Rama but found Jamadagni. They killed the sage brutally in front of his wife.

When Rama returned, he saw his mother wail in anguish at losing her husband. She cried in sorrow, beating her breast twenty-one times, and collapsed on the ground.

Seeing his father dead and his mother in this condition, Rama could not control his anger. Raising his mighty axe, Rama looked at the sky and announced loudly, 'My mother has beaten her breast twenty-one times. I will not forget the pain and agony she has suffered. I will destroy twenty-one generations of Kshatriyas to avenge this vile act.'

Rama then went to Kartavirya's palace and ruthlessly killed his sons and grandsons, thus wiping out his clan. He then went on a rampage, moving from one kingdom to another until he wiped out twenty-one generations of Kshatriyas. Finally, urged by Kashyapa, he stopped and left to the south of Aryavarta, where he spent his time in meditation.

■

The story of Kartavirya Arjuna's boon and his killing by Parashurama is a part of the *Adi Parva* in the Mahabharata. The Mahabharata epic commences with Vaishampayana narrating the story of his ancestors to Emperor Janmejaya. That is when the story of Kartavirya is narrated. It is again narrated in the Anushasana Parva, when Krishna narrates it to Yudhishtira.

Interestingly, Kartavirya appears in the Ramayana too. Once, Kartavirya blocked the flow of the river Narmada to impress his wives. This disturbed Ravana, who was busy praying to Shiva. An angry Ravana challenged Kartavirya for a fight and was humiliatingly defeated. Kartavirya then had Ravana chained and locked up.

Ravana's grandfather, the sage Pulastya, then went to meet Kartavirya. He requested Kartavirya to release his grandson. Kartavirya then released Ravana, who went back after being humiliated.

Kartavirya was a noble king who was known for his virtues. The boons he got proved to be a problem since the boons made him powerful and also arrogant. This arrogance led to a conflict with Parashurama, which led to Kartavirya's death and the destruction of thousands of Kshatriyas.

43

How Matsyagandha Became Gandhakali

The beautiful Matsyagandha rowed the boat across the Yamuna. Also known as Satyavati, she was called Matsyagandha because her bodily odour resembled that of a fish. This was natural, considering that she had been found as a child in the belly of a fish.

Matsyagandha helped her father, the king of fishermen, to earn money by rowing people across the river. Having dropped off some sages, she waited for the next passenger. A sage walked towards her. He was not an ordinary sage. His bearing and appearance revealed the fact that he was a great sage.

He was the great sage Parashara, and he walked towards the boat. Satyavati bowed to him and felt a strange sensation of respect and attraction towards the sage, such was his magnetic personality.

'I am on a pilgrimage and would like to visit the forest on the other side. Take me there, girl,' ordered the sage.

Satyavati helped the sage get into the boat and set sail. She looked around as she rowed. It had been a tiring day, and she looked forward to the day ending, so she could take some rest.

She turned to look at the sage and was surprised. The

sage was looking at her, observing her in such a way that she felt embarrassed. Satyavati was used to being looked at by men. She was beautiful, and her dress clung to her body since she worked in water throughout the day. This made her look even more attractive.

She felt embarrassed that a great sage was looking at her with lust in his eyes.

'You are so beautiful, girl. What is your name?'

'I am Satyavati, daughter of the king of fishermen.'

'I have never seen a girl as beautiful as you, even though you smell of fish. Being a sage, I have no physical desires, but today, I cannot keep my senses under control. I desire you and want you. I cannot wait and want you now!'

Satyavati was shocked. She tried to escape from the situation by saying, 'O great sage. There are so many people, including sages, at the riverbank and are watching us.'

Parashara smiled and raised his hand. Using his powers, he created a fog from his fingertips. The fog grew rapidly and soon enveloped the entire boat and the surroundings. None could see them. The sage, meanwhile, removed his robes, unable to resist the alluring beauty of Satyavati.

Satyavati would not give in to the sage so easily. She would not be an object of desire for a few moments to be thrown away.

She looked at the sage in his eyes and said confidently, 'Great sage. I am a young girl and a maiden. If I have a union with you, the world will consider me sullied. Who will marry me in the future?'

'Do not worry, Satyavati. I will use my powers to restore your virginity. This is the boon I give you. Now, do not try to resist me.'

'I will not resist you, my Lord. However, I want more boons so I am assured about my future. My body smells of fish. I want my body to emit a sweet scent. I know I will have a son with you after this act. I do not want anyone to know of this son. I also want our son to be as great and wise as you.'

'I grant all your boons,' said the sage. He reached out and embraced Satyavati, gently pushing her down on the cloth that covered the bottom of the boat.

When the sage finished, he got down at the other end of the river and went his way. The fog still enveloped the place, and Satyavati went to a nearby island. The boon of the sage came true. None would come to know about what had happened. She gave birth to a child immediately.

The power of the great sage ensured the dark-skinned child became an adult in the twinkling of an eye. She named her son Krishna Dwaipayana since he was dark (Krishna) and was born on a Dweepa (island).

Dwaipayana bowed to his mother and said, 'I understand the miraculous nature of my birth. I will now leave you. If you have any need for me in the future, just think of me, mother. I will come wherever you are.'

Dwaipayana then left from there. He would go on to study the Vedas and compile them. For his work as a compiler of the Vedas, he would be known as Veda Vyasa. After compiling the five Vedas, Vyasa then went on to write the story of his family and all that happened in the Kurukshetra War.

The work came to be known as the Mahabharata. Vyasa's student Vaishampayana narrated the story to Emperor Janmejaya, the descendant of the Pandavas. The powerful message the Mahabharata contains makes people refer to it as the fifth Veda (*Panchama Veda*).

■

The story of Satyavati and Parashara is narrated in the *Adi Parva* of the Mahabharata. This is an important milestone in the story since it has the story of the birth of the creator of the great epic.

True to his word, Vyasa came whenever Satyavati summoned him. The boons given by Parashara were significant as they led to further incidents that resulted in the birth of the Pandavas and Kauravas. A very interesting point is that Vyasa was the father of Dhritarashtra and Pandu.

The lineage of the Hastinapura throne that originated from great kings like Bharata and Kuru had changed. It was now Parashara's lineage that ruled over Hastinapura and Bharatavarsha.

44

Bheeshma Gets a Boon

Devavrata was worried. The crown prince of Hastinapura had observed that his father, the king, was listless for some time. Shantanu would meditate most of the time. Even while attending the court, he would not be attentive. The smile on his face seemed to have vanished entirely.

Devarata decided to take the issue head-on and talk to his father.

'Father,' said Devavrata, going to meet the king in his private chambers. 'I have observed that you seem to be worried. You don't seem to be your normal self. Please tell me the problem, so I can try to help. I cannot bear to see you like this. Tell me, what worries you?'

Shantanu sat quietly for a while, as though deciding whether to speak or not. Finally, he let out a deep sigh and said, 'My son, I am worried about the future of our great race. You are a great warrior known for your skills in warfare. I fear for your life, my son. What if something happens to you in a battle? The kingdom will be left with no future. After your mother, Ganga, left me, I did not take another wife. With no other son, I am now worried about the future.'

With these words, Shantanu left from there to a temple.

His father's words perturbed Devavrata. He strongly felt that there was something else that had happened.

He decided to talk to his father's key adviser. The elderly

adviser always accompanied his father wherever he went. He would probably know what made his father so worried.

The adviser was hesitant to talk, but when Devavrata was firm on wanting to know what happened, the old man decided to tell everything.

'O Prince, a few days back, your father had gone near a forest by the Yamuna River. There, he smelt a divine fragrance - a scent he had never experienced before. When he went to trace its source, he found a beautiful fisherwoman whose bodily fragrance was like nectar from a flower.'

'Who was this woman?' questioned Devavrata.

'She was Satyavati, also known as Yojanagandha, since her scent could be smelled a yojana away. She was the daughter of the king of fishermen. Your father was smitten by her beauty and proposed marriage to her.'

'Didn't she accept? What a god-sent opportunity it is for a fisher girl to become the queen of the greatest empire in the land! Is her refusal the reason for my father's grief?'

'I will explain, my prince. Our King went to meet Satyavati's father and requested him to give his daughter in marriage to him. The fisher king then put a surprising condition that he would permit the marriage only if the son born to Shantanu and Satyavati would be made the next king. Your father expressed his helplessness to agree to this condition since you were already the crown prince.'

Devarata now understood what had happened. He summoned some of the senior ministers and went to meet the king of fishermen.

Satyavati's father welcomed Devavrata and told him, 'I understand why you have come. Please understand that Satyavati is not my daughter. I only brought her up. She is the daughter of Uparichara Vasu, the great King of Chedi. She was found in a fish, along with her brother. The king decided to bring up the son and gave the daughter to me. She is a royal who belongs to the clan of King Puru.'

'I understand,' said Devavratha. 'Your daughter is noble, and deserves to be the queen of Hastinapura. I agree that the son born to my father Shantanu and your daughter should be the next king. Being the son of Ganga, and raised in an ashrama, wealth and power mean nothing to me. I will happily renounce my claim to the throne, so go ahead and agree to this marriage.'

'O great prince, you are a great follower of *dharma*. I believe your words. You are young and will be married. You will have sons. What if your sons do not respect your words? What if a son of yours prevents Satyavati's son from becoming king?'

Devavrata stood up and raised his hand to the sky. 'Listen, fisher king,' he declared. 'Let all your doubts be dispelled. Satyavati's son will be the next king, and my lineage will never challenge his rule. I vow to remain celibate for life. I will never marry or have children.'

Hearing his words, apsaras and celestials appeared in the sky, and showered flowers on Devavrata.

The celestials announced, 'He has taken a Bheeshma (terrible) oath and will henceforth be known as Bheeshma.'

Devavrata, the crown prince, thus became Bheeshma, the protector of the Hastinapura kingdom. He took Satyavati to the palace and ensured that she was married to Shantanu.

Moved by his son's devotion, Shantanu told him, 'My son. Today, you have done something that no man will do easily. For the sake of your father, you have renounced not just the throne but your future and your entire life. I am fortunate that I am your father. All the merits that I have earned in my life are yours. I use my merits to grant you a boon. No one can kill you without your permission. You will die only when you decide to do so. This is the boon I give to you.'

With this boon, Bheeshma became virtually immortal since he had the right to decide when he wanted to die. Bheeshma will always be remembered for the terrible vow he took for the sake of his father.

■

The story of Bheeshma's vow and the boon he received from his father are narrated in the *Adi Parva* of the Mahabharata. Bheeshma, the son of Ganga, became immortal thanks to the boon he secured from his father. Many kings and demons prayed to the Gods, asking for the boon of immortality, but none got this boon. Bheeshma got this boon where he could decide when to die for his devotion to his father.

Did this boon help Bheeshma or become a curse? Bheeshma had a heavy burden to carry in life. Satyavati's elder son was killed by a Gandharva. The younger son was a minor and Bheeshma functioned as regent. He then brought princesses from Kashi to get them married to Satyavati's son.

One of them, Amba, demanded that Bheeshma should marry her. When he refused, she brought the great Parashurama to intercede on her behalf. Bheeshma had to fight with his guru, Parashurama, because his vow prevented him from obeying Parashurama's order to marry Amba. In the end, Amba killed herself and was reborn as Shikhandi, who would play an important role in Bheeshma's death.

Bheeshma lived on for many years, and witnessed evil acts in the Hastinapura palace. He saw his own great-grandchildren war with each other. His vow made him loyal to the throne, and he even kept quiet when Draupadi was insulted in the royal court. He was forced to support Duryodhana in the Kurukshetra War, putting him on the side of evil.

Finally, tired of life and tired of being on the side of *adharma*, Bheeshma advised Arjuna to attack him by placing Shikhandi in front of him. Bheeshma did not fight Shikhandi. Arjuna defeated Bheeshma, striking him with arrows, causing him to fall.

Even then, Bheeshma did not give up his life. On the advice of his mother, Ganga, he awaited the sun's movement in the northern direction (*Uttarayana*). When that moment came, he gave up his life and went back to the world of the Vasus, where he had come from.

45

Vyasa's Boon and the Birth of the Kauravas

'The sage Vyasa has arrived,' announced Gandhari's maid.

The Queen got up from her seat and went to meet the sage. With the help of her maid, she washed the sage's feet and took his blessings.

'Daughter Gandhari, I have been walking for many days in the sun and am exhausted and hungry. I have come here to rest my weary feet and have food served by you.'

'It is my pleasure to serve you, great sage,' said Gandhari happily.

She then offered food to the sage, ensuring the tastiest dishes were served. Even though Gandhari had blindfolded herself, she insisted on serving the food and taking care of the great sage herself.

Once the sage had finished his meal, she made him sit on a throne. Sitting at his feet, she massaged his tired feet.

Vyasa was delighted with Gandhari's hospitality and the way she took care of him personally.

'I am pleased with you, Gandhari. You are a virtuous woman and will be a great queen of this land. It is time for you and your husband to think about giving heirs to this kingdom so that Queen Mother Satyavati will be happy. I am grateful to you for the loving way you took care of my needs. I grant you a boon that you will have a hundred sons.'

'I am grateful for your blessings, mighty sage. I would also like to have a daughter,' prayed Gandhari.

'Very well,' said Vyasa. 'You will have a hundred sons and one daughter.'

When the sage left, Gandhari conveyed news of the sage's boon to her husband, the blind king Dhritarashtra, who ruled over Hastinapura. Dhritarashtra was exultant at the thought of having a son who would be his heir. He was happier his wife would have a hundred sons to bring him glory.

Soon, Gandhari became pregnant, and all the palace ladies took good care of her. Nine months passed by, but Gandhari did not deliver. This development perturbed everyone. She still carried the foetus in her womb but could not deliver it. Soon, two years passed since she became pregnant, but yet she did not deliver.

One day, news came from the forest that Dhritarashtra's brother Pandu's wife, Kunti, had delivered a baby boy. This news upset the king, who now feared that Pandu's son would be the next king since he was the eldest. He shared his fears with Gandhari.

Frustrated by the news and distressed by her never-ending pregnancy, Gandhari lost control. She hit her belly hard, hoping she would deliver a child. Alas! The process caused her to abort the foetus from her womb, and she fell unconscious.

Everyone advised that the foetus in the shape of a mass of flesh should be thrown away. The weeping Gandhari then heard a voice that filled her with strength. It was Vyasa!

Gandhari stood up and bowed to the sage, 'Great sage, you promised me a hundred sons, but see what happened.'

'Do not worry, child,' said Vyasa. 'A boon given by me can never go wrong. Bring me a hundred and one pots. Also I want freshly prepared ghee.'

Vyasa then took out his *kamandalu* and sprinkled water on the mass of flesh that Gandhari had delivered. Through the use of his powers, he divided the mass of flesh into a hundred and one parts.

He then placed each of these parts into a pot filled with ghee. The pots were sealed and placed in a secret location.

'Wait for two more years. The results of your patient wait will definitely be fruitful. You will have a hundred sons and a daughter.'

With these words, Vyasa left from there.

After a patient wait for two years, the day of reckoning arrived. The first pot was opened and Dhritarashtra and

Gandhari's firstborn was brought out. He would be called Duryodhana. Even though there were ill-omens at the time of his birth, Dhritarashtra disregarded them and showered love on his firstborn.

One by one, the pots were opened. A total of a hundred sons were born with one daughter, Dusshala. Gandhari was happy. Her long wait had borne fruit, and she was finally a mother.

∎

The birth of the children of Gandhari and the story behind it are narrated in the *Adi Parva* of the Mahabharata. The story narrates how Vyasa was responsible for giving the boon that led to the birth of the sons of Gandhari. Vyasa was the biological father of both Dhritarashtra and Pandu. It was his boon that led to the birth of the Dharatarashtras. His boon had helped in the perpetuation of the Kuru race. It is a different matter that all the sons born had to die. Dhritarashtra's lineage ended because of the evil deeds of the eldest son.

46

The Consequences of Kunti's Boon

Kuntibhoja was happy. After a long time, the empty halls of his palace resounded with laughter. The sight of the young Pritha running around the halls laughing with the daughters of the nobles filled the king with joy.

The king had no daughter and was desperate for a girl child. When he realised that he could have no more children, he was disheartened. Kuntibhoja's sorrow gave rise to bliss when his cousin Soora permitted him to adopt his daughter Pritha.

Kuntibhoja now had a daughter to brighten his palace. He decided to rename Pritha, and soon, she began to be known as Kunti.

Kunti grew up to be a beautiful girl who was respectful of her elders, making her adopted father proud. One day, as Kunti played with her friends, she received a summons from her father. When she went to her father's chambers, Kunti saw a sage there. She fell at the sage's feet and took his blessings.

'My child, this is the great sage Durvasa,' said her father. 'He has accepted my hospitality and agreed to stay in our palace for some days. You are responsible for taking care of him. You must ensure he gets what he needs to carry out his rituals. Ensure he gets food and anything else he needs.'

Kunti dutifully agreed, and from then on served the

mighty sage with respect, taking care of every need. The sage would ask for a sweet dish. When Kunti prepared it, he would angrily reject it and demand a spicy dish. The sage was very difficult to please and created many problems for Kunti.

The princess did not lose her composure. Her upbringing had led her to believe that guests were equivalent to God. She cheerfully served the sage without getting offended by his incessant demands.

One day, Durvasa summoned Pritha. 'My child, I am pleased with your devotion. I tested you to see how steadfast you are in offering hospitality to guests, and you passed my test. I hereby grant you a boon. You are now becoming a young woman. In the future, when you need a child, you can use the boon I grant to you to summon any celestial being in the world. You will get a child through that celestial.'

Durvasa taught a mantra, which Kunti could use to summon any celestial being. He then blessed Kuntibhoja and left the palace.

Kunti was initially thrilled to get a boon from a mighty sage, but then she began to doubt its utility. She wondered how a celestial or a God would appear just by chanting a mantra.

She stood at her bedroom window one day, looking at the early morning sun. Seeing the blazing sun, she wondered if Surya, the Sun God, would come. Kunti decided this was the time to test the boon. She chanted the mantra taught by the sage.

She then saw a searing flash of light. Kunti feared she had become blind; such was the intensity of the light. She then felt a searing heat wave. In front of her stood a celestial being. Kunti could not open her eyes; such was his blazing personality. It was Surya who stood in front of her.

With great difficulty, Kunti opened her eyes. Squinting her eyes, she looked at the fiery being. In the blazing light, she saw a very handsome man. He looked at her and smiled.

'You summoned me Kunti, and I have come.'

'Please go away. I just wanted to test the sage's boon,' said Kunti, tears flowing down her cheeks.

'I cannot go away just like that. The mantra brought me here, and I will go back only after giving you a son.'

'No, no, no' cried Kunti. 'I am still a young girl. How can I have a child? What will my family think of me? Who will marry me? I don't want a son at this young age. Go away!'

'I cannot go' said Surya with an angry expression. His anger resulted in increased intensity of light and heat, causing

Kunti to close her eyes. 'If I go back, then Indra and the other gods will laugh at me.'

'Please go' said Kunti. 'I do not want any boon.'

'If you deny the boon, then I will curse you and your father,' said Surya sharply.

Weeping piteously, Kunti tried to convince Surya to go away, but to no avail. She realised that she had no option but to accept the results of the boon. She told Surya, 'I have some conditions. I do not want to lose my virginity to you, or else I will face problems in the future when I get married. I may have to abandon my son since I cannot bring him up alone. So bless my son with special powers that protect him.'

'Granted,' said Surya, who used his powers to enter Kunti using Yoga. He planted his seed inside her uterus, causing her to become pregnant, ensuring she retained her maidenhood. He then disappeared, leaving a distraught Kunti behind.

Kunti then confided in her personal maid. Her maid told her she would help hide the pregnancy.

After nine months, Kunti delivered a baby boy in secret with the help of her maid. They had taken all care to ensure no one knew Kunti was pregnant. When the child was delivered, the maid placed the boy in a basket. Both the maid and Kunti went to the river.

Weeping uncontrollably, Kunti bid goodbye to her son. There was no way she could raise him without the world knowing of her indiscretion. An unmarried princess delivering a child would cause a royal scandal that could affect her father. She would not allow her father's prestige to suffer.

She took one last look at her son, who had been born with a *kavacha* (armour) and *kundalas* (earrings). As per

Surya's blessings, the kavacha and kundala would give her son great strength and protect him. She then kissed the boy and pushed the basket, sending it floating in the river.

Kunti hid her indiscretion from the world. In due course of time, she was married to Pandu, the king of Hastinapura. Bad luck seemed to follow Kunti wherever she went. Even before she could get children from Pandu, a sage cursed him. Pandu had killed the sage when he was in union with his wife.

Before dying, the sage cursed Pandu, saying that he would die if he attempted to have a union with his wives. Shattered by the curse, Pandu abdicated his throne and left for the forest with Kunti and his second wife, Madri.

After living in the forest for a long time, one day, Pandu summoned Kunti.

'My dear wife, because of my mistake, you have been denied the opportunity of having a son by me. But we need a son to take care of us in our old age. Since I cannot give you a son, you can follow *Niyoga* and get a son from a respected Brahmana.'

Kunti then told her husband about her boon, 'When I was a young girl, I served the sage Durvasa. He gave me a boon, which would enable me to summon any God and get a son through him. It is time to use the boon now.'

Pandu was happy when he heard this. He told Kunti, 'Our eldest son should be the embodiment of *dharma*. He should be known for his righteous conduct and virtuous nature. Who better a God to invoke than Dharma, the God of justice?'

Kunti then used her boon and summoned Yama, the God of justice and death. Yama then impregnated Kunti, and she gave birth to a son. The son was named Yudhishtira, who would be known for his commitment to *dharma*.

Soon after Yudhishtira's birth, Pandu came to Kunti. 'My dear wife, we need a son who would be almighty. He should be as strong as the wind itself. Please summon the wind God Vayu and have a son by him.'

Kunti then obliged her husband and summoned Vayu. The son she got from him was named Bheema. He was so strong that, as a child, he once slipped from her hands and fell on a rock. Nothing happened to the child, but the rock was smashed into pieces.

A few months after Bheema's birth, Pandu came to Kunti.

'Dear Kunti, I always wanted a son who would be a great warrior, just like me. Just as I conquered the entire Bharatavarsha, I want a son capable of the same. He should be as skilled in archery as I am. To get such a son, we need to summon Indra, the King of the Celestials.'

Kunti again agreed with her husband's wishes. Pandu performed austerities for a year to please Indra, after which Kunti summoned Indra, who gave her a son. The day her son was born, all the Gods arrived to bless them. There were showers of flowers from the sky. Sages, apsaras, and celestials arrived to bless the boy. The son was known as Arjuna and was blessed to be as great a warrior as Rama.

Seeing that Kunti had two sons, Madri pleaded with Pandu that she should also be allowed to use Kunti's boon to get a child. Kunti reluctantly agreed. Madri used the mantra to summon the Ashwini twins and get twin sons Nakula and Sahadeva.

Kunti was angry at the misuse of her boon and decided she would never use it again. Even as Kunti enjoyed motherhood, fate dealt her a cruel blow. Pandu, in a fit of passion, attempted to have a union with Madri and fell dead.

The widowed Kunti was left with the responsibility of taking care of all five children since Madri immolated herself in the fire that burnt Pandu's body.

Kunti's boons helped her to get four sons of her own, with two more sons to look after. Sadly, she had to abandon her first son and could not give him a mother's love. While she could give a mother's love to her other sons, they did not get a father's love.

■

The story of Kunti's boon from Durvasa is narrated in the *Adi Parva* of the Mahabharata. Kunti narrated the story to Pandu. Later in the *Aranyaka Parva*, the story of Karna's birth is narrated by Vaishampayana to Janmejaya.

Undoubtedly, the boon given by Durvasa to Kunti changed the course of events in the great epic. Indeed, the history of Bharatavarsha was changed because of this boon. Without this boon, there would have probably been no Pandavas, and righteousness would be the loser.

The boon helped Kunti bring illustrious sons to the world, who would rule over the land and then rid the earth of evil. The boon also resulted in the tragic story of Karna, who was born without his birth mother's love. Kunti could not bring her first son back to the path of *dharma* and lost him in the war.

47

Draupadi Gets Five Husbands

'Draupadi will be married to all five of us,' said Yudhishtira. 'This is in accordance with our mother's words. I also believe this will be the right thing to do.'

'This is unheard of, O King,' said King Drupada. 'One man can marry many women. This is the custom prevalent. However, one woman marrying many men seems to be sinful. Is this *dharma*? Will you not be committing *adharma* by permitting this?'

'O King, *dharma* is subtle, so it is not so easy to interpret it. We are following our mother's orders, which I believe is our *dharma*. So the marriage of Draupadi to our five brothers is definitely *dharma*, have no doubt of it.'

Arjuna disguised as a brahmana had won Draupadi's hand in the *Swayamwara* organised by King Drupada. He was the only one among all the assembled kings and princes who could hit the fish on a revolving wheel by looking at its reflection in the water.

Draupadi, the daughter of the Panchala king Drupada, had garlanded him, accepting him as her husband. Drupada then summoned Arjuna and his brothers to Panchala, where Yudhishtira informed Draupadi would be wife to all the five Pandavas.

Even as Drupada was worried about whether what was being done was right, the sage Vyasa arrived.

Drupada and Yudhishtira welcomed him. After he was seated, Drupada set out to get his doubts resolved.

'O great sage. Isn't a woman marrying more than one man committing a sin? Is it *dharma* to do so?'

Vyasa then asked Yudhishtira for his opinion. Yudhishtira said, 'In the past, there was a woman named Jatila who was the wife to seven sages. There is a precedent from the past, and so I believe no sin is attached to this.'

Vyasa then took Drupada into his inner chambers to explain how Draupadi could be wife to the five Pandavas.

'O king, there once was a girl who was the daughter of a great sage. She was virtuous and beautiful but unfortunately could not find a good husband. She then began a penance to please Lord Shiva. The Lord then appeared before her and asked what she wanted.'

'Give me an accomplished husband. Give me an accomplished husband. Give me an accomplished husband. Give me an accomplished husband. Give me an accomplished husband,' asked the girl, excitedly thrilled that the Lord would grant her boon.

Shiva smiled at her and said, 'You will have five accomplished husbands.'

The girl who was shocked said, 'I only wanted one husband, great Lord, not five. Out of anxiety to get a good husband, I repeated my words five times.'

'I cannot withdraw a boon I have given,' said Shiva. 'However, you will have one husband in this life. You will have five husbands in your next life, and my boon will come true.'

'O king,' said Vyasa. 'The girl is reborn as Draupadi, who arose from the fire to be your daughter. She has a boon from Mahadeva to have five husbands, and this is ordained. She is virtuous and will remain virtuous even though she will have five husbands. Have no fear that this is *adharma*.'

Hearing these words, Drupada was happy. He then performed the marriage of Draupadi with Yudhishtira. The next day, she was given in marriage to Bheema. On the third day, she married Arjuna. On the fourth and fifth days, she was married to Nakula and Sahadeva. Thus, Draupadi had five husbands thanks to the boon from Lord Shiva.

■

The story of Draupadi's boon from her past life is narrated in the *Adi Parva* of the Mahabharata. The Pandavas, who were disguised as Brahmanas to avoid being killed by their evil cousins, were directed by none other than Vyasa to go to Panchala. Arjuna won Draupadi in the Swayamwara.

When he brought her home, he loudly told his mother to see what he had got. Kunti assumed he had brought alms and asked the brothers to share what he had got equally. This is how Draupadi ended up being the wife of five Pandavas.

Polygamy was common in those days, but polyandry was unheard of. Draupadi marrying five husbands was a unique incident. While she remained happy as wife to the five Pandavas and had five sons by them, she had to face humiliation because of this. During the infamous dice game, Karna called her a harlot because she had five husbands and justified bringing her to the hall even in a single garment or even if she was without clothes.

There is an interesting story of the sage Dirghatamas referenced in the Mahabharata. He was born blind, and since it was a burden looking after him, his wife Pradweshi threw him out by putting him adrift on a raft. The angry sage then cursed all women, saying that women could marry only once, whether their husbands were alive or dead. Probably, it was after this curse that a woman was meant to have only one husband. Draupadi's marriage to the Pandava brothers changed this narrative.

48

The Boon That Pardoned Hundred Offences

One by one, visitors came to the palace of the Chedi King Damagosha to see the newborn prince who would be king one day. The relatives and other visitors would be escorted inside the royal chambers and made to sit on chairs.

Soon, the queen Shrutakirti would come out bearing her child. She would momentarily place the child on the visitor's lap and observe what happened. She would then immediately take the child and place it on the lap of the next visitor.

This process was repeated day after day for every visitor who came. The visitors were bewildered, as to why the heir to the Chedi throne was being placed in their laps. None knew the answer. However, they knew that there was something wrong with the child.

All children were born with two hands and two eyes. The little one born to Damagosha and Shrutakirti had four hands and three eyes. The strange sight surprised the visitors and even shocked some of them. They could not express their emotions before the queen but spoke about this endlessly outside the palace.

Many of them were of the view that the child was accursed. They agreed that this was not a good sign, and the future seemed bleak for the child. They also worried about what would happen if the child with the freakish body features became king and ascended the throne.

One sunny day, even as visitors kept flocking to see the child at the invitation of the royal couple, a chariot entered the palace.

The chariot was from the palace of the Dwaraka King Ugrasena, father of Shrutakirti. In the chariot were Shrutakirti's nephews, Krishna and Balarama. The two of them had come to see the child at the invitation of their aunt Shrutakirti.

The two were welcomed and given a royal reception. When they were seated in the royal chambers, the queen came out with her baby. She greeted her cousins and enquired about everyone's health.

She then placed the baby on Balarama's lap. Even before he could play with the child, she lifted it from his lap and moved ahead. Seated next to Balarama was Krishna. She placed the baby on Krishna's lap and stood ready to lift the baby to move on to the next visitor.

Krishna smiled at the strange baby with four arms and three eyes. In an instant, the two extra arms of the baby fell off. The third eye magically disappeared, going deep into the forehead covered by skin.

Everyone in the room gasped in amazement at the extraordinary incident. The queen's attendants clapped in delight, happy that their prince was now a normal child, free from abnormal body growths.

While everyone cheered, there was only one person who wept. It was Shrutakirti.

'Why do you weep, aunt?' asked Balarama. 'Shouldn't

you be happy that your handsome son, the future king of Chedi, is now a normal child, like all other children?'

King Damagosha, who had come in, answered Balarama, 'Your aunt is worried about what Krishna will do to the child.'

'What will I do to this child? He is my cousin, and I will treat him with love and affection,' said Krishna with a smile.

'There is a story behind this,' said Damagosha. 'We were worried when our baby was born with these additional body organs. Your sister prayed relentlessly, and then we heard a voice that proclaimed that the additional organs would fall off when the baby was placed in the lap of the one who would kill him in the future.'

Shrutakirti folded her hands and looked at Krishna with tears in her eyes. 'My dear nephew, you are the one we were seeking all these days. My son lost his extra limbs and eye on your lap, so you are his killer. Spare my child, Krishna.'

Krishna got up, held his aunt's hands, and consoled her.

His aunt held Krishna's hands tightly and looked up at his eyes. 'Give me a boon, Krishna. You are no ordinary man. You killed the mighty Kamsa, and have performed many miracles. You are blessed by the Gods with magical powers. Give a boon to your aunt. I beseech you.'

Krishna smiled at his aunt and said, 'Ask whatever you want. I will not deny anything you ask.'

'Then spare my child's life. He is Shishupala, the future of this kingdom. Do not deprive us of this child born after a long time. Do not let this kingdom lose its future king. Give me a boon that you will not kill my son and pardon all the offences he may commit.'

'I will do as you say, my dear aunt. But I cannot pardon him forever. It is against the order of nature. I will pardon him for a hundred offences that he commits against me. I will forgive him, even if he commits an offence that deserves the death penalty. So do not cry and bring up the future king well so he commits no offence in the future.'

The happy queen sent off Krishna and Balarama after serving them delicious food. Alas! Her son grew up to be an evil man who became arrogant, learning of the story of his birth. He lived in the false belief that he was invincible and committed many offences.

There were many occasions when Shishupala offended Krishna and came into conflict with him. Each time, Krishna pardoned him. Shishupala kept indulging in one vile act after the other. He abducted the future wife of the noble Babhru. He ill-treated his uncle Karusha and abducted the Vishala princess Bhadra. Shishupala even attacked Dwaraka, causing widespread destruction.

Krishna did not act against Shishupala, respecting the boon he had given to the Chedi king's mother. What Shishupala did not know was that Krishna was keeping a count of all the offences committed by Shishupala.

Many years later, Yudhishtira performed the Rajasuya yajna. His brothers set out in the four directions to add kingdoms to Yudhishtira's rule. Bheema was the Pandava who reached Chedi. The clever Shishupala realised he could not defeat Bheema, and welcomed him heartily.

Shishupala's hospitality pleased Bheema. Shishupala offered tributes and agreed to accept Yudhishtira's rule and participate in the Rajasuya yajna. Accordingly, Shishupala attended the yajna.

When the time came to honour the guests, a question arose as to who should be honoured first.

Bheeshma then stood up and said, 'O Yudhishtira. Have no doubt in your mind. The one who deserves to be honoured first is none other than Krishna. He is like the sun among the stars in the assembly hall. Honour him, for he deserves it for his energy and valour.'

Yudhishtira happily honoured Krishna, heeding the words of the grandsire. Even as Yudhishtira honoured Krishna, there was a voice that interrupted.

'Stop, Krishna does not deserve this honour. He is not even a king, so why is he being honoured? Honouring him is an insult to all the kings assembled here. When the preceptor Drona is here, how can you honour Krishna? I reject this act.'

It was Shishupala who objected and walked out of the hall. Yudhishtira ran behind him and brought him back, requesting him to listen to Bheeshma.

Bheeshma said, 'Krishna is wiser than all the Brahmanas and learned in the Vedas. He is stronger than all the warriors and is valorous, modest, and supreme in all deeds. He is the Supreme Being and worthy of all worship. It is only a childlike Shishupala who will object out of ignorance.'

An angry Shishupala retorted, 'You are an old man who does not know *dharma*. Why did you abduct Amba and then desert her? Your claim of being celibate is fake. This Krishna used deceit to kill the brave Emperor Jarasandha. Karna is greater than Krishna. Bahlika, Drona, Ashwathama, and Shalya are greater than this cowherd. You are truly a shameful one who lives at the pleasure of other Lords.'

Some kings supported Shishupala even while a furious Bheema had to be restrained from attacking Shishupala.

Bheeshma then announced, 'Krishna has been honoured. If any of you do not like to live, challenge Krishna for a fight. Stop these empty words.'

Shishupala then shouted loudly, 'I challenge Krishna. I will kill him today, and if any of the Pandavas support him, I will kill them too. Rukmini was mine, and this vile Krishna took her away from me. What kind of man is he whose wife was someone else's first?'

Even as there was a tumult in the hall, Krishna, who was silent all this while, stood up.

'This Shishupala has committed vile offences against women and even stole my father's horses. He killed the royals of Bhoja and has many sins against his name. I forgave him all these days because of the boon I had granted to his mother. His act of insolence and transgression today has led to him committing more than a hundred offences. He will now die at my hands.'

Krishna then raised his finger, and the Sudarshana Chakra appeared on it. Spinning his finger, he released the discus that flew through the air towards Shishupala. Even as the horrified Chedi king watched, the discus severed his head, sending it flying in the air. Shishupala had committed one offence too many and now lay dead.

■

The story of Krishna's boon to Shishupala's mother is narrated in the *Sabha Parva* of the Mahabharata. Bheeshma narrated this story to the assembled kings and guests. Krishna then revealed that Shisupala had crossed a hundred offences and hence would be killed.

A boon is given as protection. Shishupala did not understand the protection offered. Even after being offered a limit of a hundred offences, he arrogantly committed one sin after the other, until he lost the protection of the boon. After Shishupala's death, his son Dhrishtaketu became the king of Chedi. Dhrishtaketu supported the Pandavas during the Kurukshetra war.

49

Dhritarashtra Offers Boons to Draupadi

'This is my oath. I will kill all the hundred sons of Dhritarashtra to avenge the insult to Draupadi,' roared Bheema with his huge hands in the air, his nostrils flared and chest heaving.

The terrible sight caused Gandhari to shake in fear. She had just entered the hall where the dice game was going on after hearing of the terrible happenings.

The dice game that was played for recreation had become serious when Yudhishtira staked his empire. With the wily Shakuni casting the dice on behalf of Duryodhana, Yudhishtira's loss was assured.

The Emperor of Yudhishtira had lost everything in the dice game, including his empire. In desperation, he staked his brothers one by one and lost them. He then staked himself and lost. After being provoked by Shakuni, he staked his wife, Draupadi, and lost her.

Draupadi was dragged to the hall by Dusshasana, who then attempted to disrobe her. Dharma saved her, but a furious Bheema vowed to tear Dusshasana's chest and drink his blood.

Duryodhana then mockingly asked Draupadi to sit on his thigh since she was his slave. That was when Bheema took an oath not just to break Duryodhana's thigh in battle, but also to kill all the sons of Dhritarashtra and Gandhari.

Hearing these words, Gandhari was shaken. The words had made Dhritarashtra's heart skip a beat. He knew how powerful Bheema was and had no doubt he would fulfil his vow.

Gandhari then pleaded with Dhritarashtra to intervene and prevent a disaster. The blind king, who had refused to listen to the advice of his Prime Minister Vidura, was now jolted awake, realising the seriousness of Bheema's vow.

And then evil omens began to be heard. Jackals howled in the distance, and donkeys brayed. Birds of various kinds uttered terrible sounds.

Dhritarashtra then decided that he had to do something.

He addressed Draupadi, who lay on the floor weeping in humiliation and rage.

'Daughter Draupadi, my son Duryodhana, is evil-minded. He has humiliated a woman who is the wife of others. You are a chaste woman who follows *dharma*, and did not deserve this treatment. I need to atone for my son's sinful act, so ask any boon you want. I will grant it.'

Draupadi then took a deep breath to compose herself. She wiped the tears from her face using the back of her hand. Standing up, she walked towards the king and bowed to him.

'O King, if you desire to give me a boon, then liberate my husband, Yudhishtira. I cannot tolerate the idea of him being a slave. My son Prativindhya will be known as the son of a slave, which is something I cannot bear.'

'I grant this boon. The wise and virtuous Yudhishtira will no longer be a slave. Daughter Draupadi, ask for one more boon. You deserve another boon to compensate for all the humiliation you suffered.'

'O King, I ask that my husbands, Bheema, Arjuna, Nakula, and Sahadeva be liberated, along with their weapons and chariots. None of them should be slaves.'

'I grant your boon. None of your husbands are slaves anymore. You are the best among all my daughters-in-law. Ask for one more boon. I will give you all that you want.'

'O King, greed will destroy *dharma*. The scriptures say that Kshatriyas and their wives can ask for only two boons. I do not wish to ask for more boons. My husbands are now free. They will earn riches and prosperity through their skills. I do not desire any boon.'

Dhritarashtra addressed Yudhishtira and said, 'O dear son of Pandu, I know the actions of Duryodhana have been hurtful. Forgive him, for my sake. You know *dharma*, and I know you will follow *dharma*, and will not keep hatred in your heart. I return your kingdom and all that you lost. Go back to your kingdom and live happily by following *dharma*. Show love for your brothers and do not have anger or hatred for them.'

Yudhishtira bowed to the king, and returned to his kingdom with his brothers and wife. The sordid episode of the dice game had ended.

Little did Yudhishtira know Duryodhana would again force the blind king to bring back the Pandavas to the assembly. They would be forced to play another game of dice, where they would lose everything and be sent to exile.

■

The story of the infamous dice game is part of the *Sabha Parva* in the Mahabharata. After being humiliated, Draupadi is given boons, but she chooses to go by dharma and only asks for two boons. She does not even ask that she be liberated as an enslaved person, but asks for her husbands to be freed.

Dhritarashtra's boons did not help the Kauravas or change the future. The reason was that he once again listened to his evil son and called back the Pandavas for a second game of dice. The insult to a woman had sealed the fate of the Kauravas. Thirteen years after the game, a great war took place where Bheema fulfilled his oath and killed all hundred sons of Dhritarashtra.

The Kuru clan was wiped out and millions of soldiers were killed. Widespread death and devastation occurred, all because of the blind affection of the king for his evil son and the insult caused to a virtuous woman.

50

Akshaya Patra—the Vessel of Plenty

'How will we feed everyone? This is my biggest worry,' said Draupadi to Yudhishtira, who sat thoughtfully before their house in the forest.

'Yes, the same thought occurred to me. We have a large entourage with us. Many Brahmanas have accompanied us to carry out the daily rituals. Many other aides have accompanied us. They have come with us out of love for us and are ready to share the hardships of forest life. The least we can do is offer them a filling meal each day.'

The Pandavas were in exile in the forest at Dwaitavana after they lost the game of dice. They were cheated due to Shakuni's wily deception. As per the terms agreed before, they had to spend twelve years in exile, with an additional year of exile in disguise without being identified.

With the Pandavas came many well-wishers. Yudhishtira intended to perform rituals during their stay in the forest. So their chief priest, Dhaumya, and other Brahmanas accompanied them. The Pandavas had left their kingdom with nothing. They would get in the forest all they needed to stay and perform rituals. The problem was food!

Just then, Dhaumya came there. Yudhishtira told him about their concern.

Dhaumya advised him, 'The sun is the sustainer of life. The sun's light is what helps plants grow leaves, roots, and fruits. It is the light of the sun that fills our lives with hope for the future. The sun will provide food. Pray to Surya, and he will give you a solution.'

Yudhishtira followed the priest's advice and prayed long to the giver of the light. Soon, Surya appeared before him.

'O Yudhishtira, I will help solve your problems. I will give you the food you need for your twelve-year stay in the forest. I will give you the Akshaya Patra, a vessel that will provide you with unlimited food. Whether it is fruits, vegetables, roots, or meat, you will get all that you need.'

Yudhishtira bowed to Surya and thanked him for his gift that solved his problem.

Yudhishtira then went to the kitchen after taking the blessings of Dhaumya. He then prepared food using the vessel given by Surya. Once the food was prepared, it became inexhaustible. Yudhishtira then fed the Brahmanas. He then fed his brothers and the others.

Yudhishtira then ate the remaining food. What was left was finally eaten by Draupadi. The Pandavas thus spent their exile in the forest without worrying about food.

■

The story of Surya giving the gift of inexhaustible food is narrated in the *Aranyaka Parva* of the Mahabharata. While the critical edition of the Mahabharata does not use the word 'Akshaya Patra', some other editions and translations use this term.

The Akshaya Patra denotes unlimited food. Some editions have an additional story. While gifting the vessel, Surya told Yudhishtira that the food would remain inexhaustible until Draupadi ate. The moment Draupadi ate, the food would be exhausted until the next day.

Everyone knew this, including Duryodhana. He then hatched a plan to embarrass the Pandavas. The plan came to his mind when the sage Durvasa visited Hastinapura. The sage was known for his short temper and propensity to curse anyone who offended him.

Duryodhana took good care of the sage and pleased him. When Durvasa was happy, Duryodhana requested that he meet the Pandavas in the forest and bless them. He requested Durvasa to go in the evening hour, knowing that Draupadi would have finished her meal by then. The pleased Durvasa agreed to Duryodhana's demand.

Durvasa then reached the place where the Pandavas stayed. Yudhishtira invited him for a meal. He had come with hundreds of his disciples, and they went to the river to bathe before eating.

Draupadi was upset because she had finished eating her food.

'What do I do now? There is no food, and the sage will be here soon. If I do not offer him food, he will curse me. Only Krishna can do something. How I wish he were here!' thought Draupadi.

'Panchali,' said a voice near the door, making Draupadi run towards the door.

It was Krishna. No sooner had Draupadi thought about Krishna than he was there.

'Krishna, I am in a desperate situation. You must help me.'

'What is this, Draupadi? Is this how you treat guests? I am hungry. Offer me food,' said Krishna, with a twinkle in his eyes.

'Don't joke, Krishna. My situation is dire. There is no food, and I am worried,' cried Draupadi.

'Bring me the vessel; there could probably be some food.'

Draupadi brought the Akshaya Patra and showed it to

Krishna, who peered inside the vessel. There was a single grain in it. Krishna took out the grain and ate it.

'Ah! My stomach is full,' said Krishna, smiling at Draupadi.

Even as Krishna said these words, Durvasa and his disciples felt their stomachs full and bloated. They realised that they could not eat even a single grain, and quietly left.

Krishna thus saved Draupadi, preventing the Pandavas from being exposed to the curse of Durvasa. The story also conveys that devotion can help one solve any problem.

The Akshaya Patra is a very important concept in Indian tradition and is associated with food and service to others. This is why the well-known ISKCON temple has named its mid-day meal scheme Akshaya Patra. Through this scheme, tens of thousands of school students are given free mid-day meals to fill their stomachs and to motivate them to come to school and study.

51

Arjuna Gets the Celestial Weapons

'Listen to me, Yudhishtira,' said the sage Vyasa. 'The time will come when you need to fight a war to regain your kingdom. Arjuna will then help you overcome your enemies. For him to succeed, he needs celestial weapons from the Gods. He must go to the abode of the Gods and seek these divine weapons.'

Yudhishthira understood the importance of Vyasa's words and called Arjuna. He instructed him to cross the Gandhamadhana Mountains and meet Indra, the Lord of the celestials, to obtain divine weapons.

Arjuna then set off, taking long strides. It took him many days as he walked through forests and mountains. Finally, he reached the mighty Gandhamadhana Mountains. It was a most arduous journey crossing the majestic mountains, but Arjuna was determined to reach his destination.

The moment he crossed the mountains, he knew he would reach the gates of Indraloka. Ordinary men could not cross this mountain, but Arjuna was not only strong but also virtuous. This helped him cross the mountains without difficulty.

As he moved towards the gates of Indraloka, he saw an old man seated below a tree. The old man was an ascetic who blazed with the merits of the austerities he had performed.

Opening his eyes, he asked Arjuna, 'Who are you? Why

are you coming here with weapons? There is no place for weapons here. Return to where you came from?'

'Respected sire,' said Arjuna, bowing before the ascetic. 'I come here to meet the Lord of the celestials.'

'Humans cannot go beyond this point. Give up your foolish quest and return from where you came.'

'No, I will not. I have assured my brother that I will meet Indra and obtain the secret of celestial weapons from him. I am determined to complete my mission, come what may.'

The old man smiled, and his form transformed into a majestic figure in royal robes, radiant as a thousand suns.

'I am Indra. I am the one you come to meet. I am not just the king of celestials, but also your father. Tell me what you seek?'

Arjuna took Indra's blessings by touching his feet. He asked Indra for celestial weapons.

Indra replied, 'You have to first take the blessings of Lord Shiva. Once he blesses you, the secrets of the celestial weapons will be revealed to you.'

Having said these words, Indra vanished. Arjuna then decided to go to the Kailasa Mountains. He crossed the Himalayas, spending many days on his quest to reach Kailasa.

Arjuna reached the peak of the Himalayas and meditated on the Lord of Lords Shiva. He constructed a Shiva linga and prayed to Mahadeva Shiva. He spent many months performing rigorous austerities, determined to achieve his goal.

Every day, he would perform his morning rituals and then pray to the Lord before resuming his austerities. One day, as he was praying before the Shiva linga, he heard a huge commotion.

He heard snorting sounds and opened his eyes. He saw a huge boar with sharp tusks charging towards him. Getting up instantly, he picked up the Gandiva and fixed an arrow to it. Even before the boar could take a few steps towards him, he released the arrow.

Just as the arrow was about to hit the boar, another arrow came from behind it, striking it on its neck. The boar fell dead.

Arjuna was irritated that someone else had killed the boar he had targeted. He looked around and saw a Kirata standing before him, twirling his moustache. Behind the hunter-chief was a beautiful lady who looked at her husband in admiration. Hundreds of tribals cheered their leader for killing the boar.

Kirata's wife looked at Arjuna mockingly and said, 'My husband is so skilled in archery. He killed the boar in an instant.'

Arjuna laughed at hearing these words. 'It was my arrow that killed the boar. Your husband committed a sin by shooting the boar that I shot at. I have every right to punish him for his act.'

The Kirata smiled, looking at Arjuna from top to bottom. 'You boast a lot, you puny man. I am the greatest archer in the world. Don't stand before me lest I kill you. Go away from here.'

'You dare say this to me?' said Arjuna, fixing an arrow to his bow. 'I challenge you to a duel. I will defeat you and teach you a lesson you won't forget.'

Even before Arjuna could release his arrow, the Kirata had fixed an arrow to his bow and released it. Arjuna released his arrow, and both arrows smashed into each other in mid-air.

A fierce duel broke out with Arjuna, releasing a shower of arrows. The Kirata effortlessly destroyed every arrow Arjuna flung at him.

A furious Arjuna kept releasing one arrow after the arrow but could not defeat the Kirata. Arjuna's fingers moved to his inexhaustible quiver, and he was shocked to see that it had run out of arrows.

A stunned Arjuna was amazed by what had happened. Not knowing what to do, he tried to grab the Kirata with the string of his bow. The Kirata laughed at Arjuna, and plucking the Gandiva from his hands, threw it away.

Arjuna then pulled out his sword and struck the Kirata on his head. Any person in the world would be dead, but the Kirata stood like a rock even as the sword broke in two. Arjuna then charged at the Kirata, grappling with him. The Kirata effortlessly lifted Arjuna and threw him on the ground.

A humiliated Arjuna lay on the ground, unable to believe how an ordinary tribal hunter had defeated the greatest warrior in the world. He looked up and saw the Shiva linga. Determined to avenge his humiliation, Arjuna looked around and saw flowers in a bush.

He quickly strung a garland of flowers using the vine from a creeper even as the Kirata stood watching with his hands on his hips. Arjuna placed the garland on the Shiva linga and prayed to Shiva to grant him strength.

He then got up and roared loudly, 'I now have the blessings of Mahadeva. Let us see who can stop me now.'

He charged towards the Kirata but stopped mid-way, his mouth open wide in amazement. On the Kirata's neck was the same garland he had placed on the linga. That was when he realised the truth.

The Kirata was none other than Mahadeva, who had come to test him, and his wife was Parvati, the mother of the world.

Arjuna fell at Shiva's feet, placing his forehead on the Lord's feet.

'Get up, Arjuna,' said Shiva, assuming his actual form. The Goddess stood next to Shiva, smiling at Arjuna.

'I am pleased with your valour and steadfastness,' said Mahadeva. 'I grant you what you have come for. I grant you my all-powerful weapon, Pashupata that even Indra and Varuna do not have. I also grant you the use of the Brahmashira missile. With these weapons, there will be none in the world who can defeat you. Use these weapons wisely against worthy opponents.'

The Lord then placed his hand on Arjuna's head. Arjuna felt energy surge through him. Shiva then left from there with Parvati and his followers.

Indra then arrived in a golden chariot and took Arjuna to the world of the celestials, where he stayed for a long time. Indra blessed Arjuna with celestial weapons, including the Vajra. Varuna, Agni, Yama, and other gods also gave many mighty armaments to Arjuna.

Arjuna had achieved his mission. He had set out on a quest for celestial weapons and had earned it thanks to his dedication. He was now confident that when the time came to use it, he would prove his abilities and help his family win back their lost empire.

This story is narrated in the *Aranyaka Parva* of the Mahabharata, where Vaishampayana tells Janamejaya of Arjuna's journey to obtain celestial weapons—a pivotal moment that ensured victory in the Kurukshetra War.

52

How Jayadratha's Boons Failed to Help Him

'Shave his head,' said Draupadi. 'Don't shave it fully. Shave it partially and release him.'

Bheema chuckled with delight. Pulling out a knife, he grabbed Jayadratha's hair and shaved it. He shaved out most of his hair, leaving just five tufts of hair on his head.

Bheema looked at the results in appreciation, laughing heartily at Jayadratha's humiliation.

'You wretch,' said Bheema, grabbing Jayadratha by the throat and lifting him in the air.

'Being the husband of our uncle Dhritarashtra's daughter Dusshala, you are our brother-in-law. Our wife, Draupadi, is like a sister to you. Yet you dared to abduct her to satisfy your lust. You are fortunate that Yudhishtira is ever forgiving. If he had not restricted me, I would have broken your bones and sent your body back to your kingdom in pieces.'

Yudhishtira told Jayadratha, 'I spared you because Dusshala is our sister. I cannot be the cause of her losing her husband. Go and lead a better life and give up your lustful behaviour.'

'Yes, we have punished him enough by shaving his head. Let's now set him free,' said Draupadi.

Bheema threw Jayadratha down on the ground. The

King of Sindhu got up and limped away, his head bent low in humiliation. Unable to control his lustful behaviour, he tried to abduct Draupadi when he saw her alone but was humiliatingly defeated by Arjuna and Bheema.

With his head shaved in this way, there was no way he could return to his kingdom. He could die rather than be humiliated in front of his citizens. Jayadratha wondered if he should end his life. He then decided that he had to avenge this humiliation.

He went to the forests and threw away his armour and royal garments. Sitting on a rock wearing bark, he meditated on Lord Shiva. With a single-minded focus, he performed austerities for years. Pleased with his devotion, Shiva appeared in front of him.

'I am pleased with your devotion, Jayadratha. Ask for a boon,' said the Lord Mahadeva.

'O great lord. I want the power to defeat the five Pandavas in battle.'

Shiva smiled at Jayadratha. 'None can defeat Arjuna, who is blessed by me and has Krishna with him. You can defeat the Pandavas, except Arjuna, but only once.'

Blessing Jayadratha, Shiva vanished. A happy Jayadratha returned to his kingdom. He met his father, Vriddhakshatra, and told him about the boon from Shiva.

Vriddhakshatra was happy to know that his son had pleased Mahadeva. He told his son, 'My son, the Pandavas will not spare you. If anything happens to you, it will be the end of this kingdom. I have performed austerities for years and have earned merit from it. I use all my merits to grant you a boon. This boon will protect your life.'

Pouring water from a *kamandalu* in his right palm,

Vriddhakshatra closed his eyes in prayer.

He opened his eyes, sprinkled the water on Jayadratha's head and said, 'This is my boon to you. Anyone who causes your head to fall on the ground will die with his head shattered into a hundred pieces.'

Jayadratha bowed to his father. He was happy that he had two boons. His father's boon had made him virtually immortal in battle. Anyone who killed him would cause his body and head to fall to the ground. The moment that happened, his killer would also die. This would dissuade anyone from killing him.

He would use the boon from Lord Shiva at the right moment and defeat the Pandavas. He knew that the moment would come very soon.

Jayadratha was right. A few years later, the Great War occurred between the Pandavas and the Kauravas, with Jayadratha on the side of the Kauravas.

On the thirteenth day of the war, Drona ensured Arjuna was taken away from the battlefield by the Trigartas. He then formed the Chakravyuha that none could penetrate. Drona planned to use the formation to defeat the Pandavas and capture Yudhishtira, thus ending the war.

Drona did not know that Abhimanyu, Arjuna's son, knew how to break into the wheel formation. But Abhimanyu did not know how to break out of the formation. Yudhishtira then assured Abhimanyu they would follow him inside the formation once he broke into it.

Abhimanyu then smashed open the Chakravyuha and entered it. He created havoc in the Kaurava forces all day. The problem was that he had to fight alone. Yudhishtira, Bheema, and the other Pandavas tried to follow Abhimanyu into the Chakravyuha, but were stopped by Jayadratha.

Jayadratha invoked Shiva's boon, and used it to hold off the Pandavas throughout the day. As a result, Abhimanyu had to fight alone the entire day. The Kauravas then used deceit and killed him by breaking the rules of the war, with Karna cutting his bow from behind.

After the day's battle was over, Arjuna returned from his battle with the Trigartas. When he came to know about what happened, he was furious. He took an oath to kill Jayadratha the next day before sunset, failing which he would kill himself.

The Kauravas sensed a golden opportunity, and Drona used a combination of three formations to defend Jayadratha. But no one could stop Arjuna. Guided by Krishna, Arjuna smashed apart Drona's formation, and slaughtered lakhs of Kaurava soldiers.

Finally, before sunset, Arjuna killed Jayadratha. Krishna knew of Vriddhakshatra's boon. On his advice, Arjuna beheaded Jayadratha and, using a powerful arrow, sent Jayadratha's head flying through the air. He guided the arrow, so it reached the place where Vraddhakshatra was performing his evening rituals.

The head of Jayadratha landed on his father's lap. Seeing his son's head, the shocked Vraddhakshatra stood up, making the head fall to the ground. Since it was Vraddhakshatra who was responsible for his son's head falling on the ground, his head shattered into a hundred pieces. Both father and son lay dead.

■

This is the story of a boon that did not help the person who got the boon. The story of Shiva's boon to Jayadratha is narrated in the *Aranyaka Parva* of the Mahabharata. The Drona Parva has the narration of Jayadratha's killing.

Most books, TV shows, and movies show Krishna causing an eclipse to help Arjuna kill Jayadratha. This is a myth, and is not a part of the Vyasa Mahabharata.

This story is a rare example where a person received two boons, including one from Mahadeva. The boons did not help Jayadratha since he lost his life in the end. It shows how a boon would fail to yield results when it is misused or obtained by an evil person.

53

How Savitri Got the Better of Yama

'So, what have you decided, daughter?' asked Ashwapathi, the king of Kekeya Kingdom the land of fine horses.

'I have made my choice, father. I trust you will accept it,' said Ashwapathi's daughter, Savitri.

'That is why I allowed you to choose your own husband. I trust your intelligence. You are, after all, born with the blessings of the God Savitr. Whatever you do is right. You have travelled the length and breadth of the land and seen many young men. Who do you choose for your husband?'

'I choose Satyavan, the son of Dyumatsena.'

'Dyumatsena! I have heard this name. Wasn't he the king of Shalva? I heard he was deposed as king and that he is blind.'

'Yes, father, Dyumatsena is aged and blind. He lives in a small hut in the forest with his wife and his son Satyavan.'

'I can't believe it, Savitra! There are so many princes, nobles, and warriors. Yet you chose the poor son of a king without a kingdom. What did you see in him that you selected a man who lives in poverty in the forest?'

'Father,' said Savitri. 'He has been named aptly. He is known for his truthfulness and his devotion to his parents. He is wise and the most virtuous man in the world. I choose virtue over wealth, kingdom, and valour. I trust you will respect my choice.'

Just then, the sage Narada arrived in Ashwapathi's palace. The king bowed to him and welcomed him. After the sage was seated, Ashwapathi told him about Savitri's choice.

'O my dear child, what a decision you have taken!' said the sage, his face downcast.

'What happened, great sage? Is he not the right choice for my daughter?'

'O king,' said Narada with a smile on his face. 'Satyavan is as handsome as the Ashwini twins. He is as generous as the great king Rantideva. Satyavan is as devoted and virtuous as Shibi, who cut his own flesh to save a dove. He is a devoted son and known for his good conduct.'

'Then why do you question my daughter's decision, revered sage?' asked the worried king.

'There is one problem. Satyavan's life span on this earth is short. One year from this day, his life will come to an end. It is ordained, and none can change this. If your daughter marries him, she will become a widow in one year.'

'My daughter will change her decision,' said the king.

'I will not, father. I have made my decision. In my mind, I have accepted him as my husband. I cannot accept someone else. He is my husband, irrespective of what happens in the future.'

Narada then advised the king, 'Your daughter has made up her mind. Do not stop her. He is an ideal husband. As far as the future is concerned, whatever is ordained in your daughter's fate will happen.'

With a heavy heart, Ashwapathi agreed. He went and

met Dyumatsena, and with his approval, got his daughter Savitri married to Satyavan.

Savitri happily shed her royal robes and ornaments. Dressed in bark and other garments, she lived in the hut with her husband and in-laws. She took care of her in-laws, treating them with respect. Satyavan was happy seeing the virtuous nature of his wife.

Savitri kept count of the days with trepidation. Soon, the day of his death came close. Three days before the destined day, Savitri began to observe severe austerities. She fasted and remained standing day and night, refusing to rest.

Three days passed in this way. On the ill-fated day, Satyavan set out to the forest with an axe to get wood. Savitri said she would come with him.

'Dear Savitri,' said Satyavan. 'You are observing intense austerities and have become thin and weak. You do not have the strength to come to the forest. Stay here. I will be back soon.'

'No, my dear husband,' said Savitri. 'Do not dissuade me. I may be physically weak, but I am mentally strong. I will come with you wherever you go.'

Satyavan had to agree and took Savitri to the woods. Savitri walked behind her husband, her heart racing, fearing the worst.

Suddenly, Satyavan turned to his wife and held her hand. 'Savitri, I am feeling a terrible pain in my chest. I am exhausted and am not able to stand. I will rest for a while.'

With these words, and even before Savitri could do anything, Satyavan collapsed and fell dead. Savitri was shattered to see her dead husband. The worst had come true. She placed her husband's head on her lap and sat silently, not knowing what to do.

She then saw a bright light. Someone was walking towards her. It was a celestial being seated on a huge buffalo. In his hand was a noose. It was Yama, the God of death.

'O Yama,' said Savitri. 'I have heard that your assistants come to take the souls of dead people to the other world. Why have you come yourself?'

'Satyavan is such a virtuous man that I decided to come myself.'

With these words, Yama flung his noose. It coiled around Satyavan's neck. He pulled the noose, and Satyavan's soul came out of his body. Yama took Satyavan's soul and left.

Savitri ran behind Yama. Seeing her, he said, 'O wise lady, go back and ensure Satyavan's last rites are complete. Do not be foolish enough to follow me.'

'O, Lord of death. I am a dutiful wife. It is my *dharma* to go wherever my husband goes. I will come with you since you take my husband.'

'I am pleased with your thoughts about *dharma*. I grant you a boon. Ask anything you want except the life of your husband,' said Yama.

'Then let my father-in-law regain his eyesight and become strong and healthy.'

'I grant your boon,' said Yama, raising his hands in blessing. He turned to leave but was surprised to see Savitri follow him again. He questioned if she was not exhausted.

Savitri told Yama, 'There is no exhaustion because I follow my virtuous husband. Following the virtuous is the right thing to do in this world.'

Yama smiled at Savitri. 'I am pleased with your wisdom. Ask any boon except the life of your husband.'

'I then ask you to restore my father-in-law's lost kingdom.'

'Granted,' said Yama and left, but Savitri continued to follow him.

When questioned, she told Yama, 'Great Lord, *dharma* is kindness towards others. You are righteous and dharma itself. So, you should show kindness even to those ill-disposed to you.'

'Your understanding of *dharma* pleases me. Ask for another boon.'

'My father, Ashwapathi has no sons to continue his lineage. Please grant him a hundred sons.'

'Granted, and now go back. You have come too far.'

'There is no distance when I am with my husband. You are the king of *dharma* and are affectionate towards those who are virtuous.'

Yama was happy hearing her words and said, 'I am impressed with your words and have never heard such wisdom from humans. I grant you a fourth boon. Ask anything other than your husband's life.'

'Then I ask for a hundred sons born to me to continue Satyavan's lineage.'

'Granted,' said Yama.

'O, Great Lord. You have granted me a hundred sons through Satyavan but are taking him away to the other world. How can I have sons without my husband? Your words can never become false, so please give me back my husband.'

Yama smiled at Savitri and said, 'I am pleased with your steadfastness, wisdom, and presence of mind. Take back your husband's life.'

With these words, Yama disappeared.

Savitri ran to the place where Satyavan's body lay. Even as she reached, she saw him get up and rub his eyes, as though waking from sleep.

She hugged her husband in delight. When they returned to their home, they saw the people of Shalva there. The citizens had thrown out the usurper and invited Dyumatsena back to the kingdom.

Dyumatsena, who had regained his eyesight, accepted. He returned as king and ruled for many years before handing over the kingdom to Satyavan. Savitri had a hundred sons who were wise and noble. Her father had a hundred sons who were known as the Malavas, named after her mother Malavi.

■

The story of Satyavan and Savitri is one of the most famous stories known across the length and breadth of the country. Wives everywhere worship Savitri and perform austerities in her name, praying for the longevity of their husbands' lives. The famous story is narrated in the *Aranyaka Parva* of the Mahabharata. The sage Markandeya narrates this story to the Pandavas.

Markandeya tells this story and compares Savitri with Draupadi. He tells Yudhishtira that Draupadi is as virtuous as Savitri. The sage predicts that Draupadi will help Yudhishtira get back his kingdom just as Savitri helped her husband get back his life and kingdom. This incident occurs after Draupadi is abducted by Jayadratha and rescued. Hearing the sage's story, the Pandavas are comforted.

Savitri has become a household name in India. She is associated with a wife who protects her husband's life and health. Savitri is a word used to denote a dutiful wife. Some people refer to this as a sign of patriarchy where a wife's job is supposed to be only to take care of her husband.

This is entirely far from the truth. Savitri is a classic example of an independent woman who lived thousands of years ago. She had the freedom to go throughout the country and select her husband herself. She made an independent choice, even though her father opposed it.

She stuck to her decision and used her wisdom and quick thinking to save her husband from death. Savitri is the perfect example of a strong, bold, and wise woman. She should be an inspiration for all those who want to be independent and intelligent.

54

Indra Converts a Curse into a Boon

'Go and meet Urvashi,' said Chitrasena, the king of the Gandharvas.

'The famous apsara, known for her beauty and charm?' questioned Arjuna.

'Yes, I suggest you go to her chambers in the palace and meet her?'

'But I don't understand why?'

'You are a prince and a future king. You are a Kshatriya with many wives. You must learn how to deal with beautiful women. Spending time with Urvashi will help you.'

'I don't think it is necessary,' said Arjuna doubtfully.

Chitrasena clapped Arjuna on his shoulders and said, 'Trust me, it is in your best interests that you spend some time with her.'

Arjuna had to accept the advice of his host, Chitrasena, with whom he had stayed for a long time.

He set off to Urvashi's chambers and was led in by her servant.

He was made to sit on a huge throne and awaited the famous danseuse.

He heard the sounds of jangling anklets and turned to see Urvashi approach. Undoubtedly, she was one of the most beautiful women in the world. She had big expressive eyes with long eyelashes. Her lips were full, and her smile was inviting. Her fair complexion enhanced her beauty.

She had the most perfect body, her curves undulating as she walked towards Arjuna, holding a golden goblet. It was no wonder many kings and sages had lost their senses seeing her beauty.

She walked over to Arjuna and smiled at him. He smiled back and accepted the glass of wine offered to him. He was unsure if the wine was more intoxicating or the grace of her presence.

Taking a deep breath, Arjuna composed himself and drank the wine in a gulp.

She laughed, a sound that resembled that of a brook. Her very laugh could make men go mad.

'That's not the way to drink wine. You should drink it a sip at a time and relish the taste. Relish the wine and enjoy life. Just as you enjoy the wine, relax and enjoy my beauty.'

'Pardon me,' said Arjuna, keeping the glass on a side table and getting up.

Urvashi pushed him back onto the throne and sat on his lap.

'Great warrior, it is not enough to show your prowess on the battlefield. You need to show me how strong you are,' said the nymph, leaning toward Arjuna, touching his lips with her fingers.

Arjuna closed his eyes and took a deep breath. He thought of Draupadi waiting for him to return from the world of celestials. He gently held Urvashi by her waist, making her gasp. With a quick movement, he lifted her in the air. Getting up from the throne, he gently placed her on the throne.

She sat there, bewildered by Arjuna's reaction.

Arjuna bowed to her and said, 'I appreciate your interest in me. But for me, you are like a mother.'

'What do you mean?' asked Urvashi, a frown on her face.

'You were the wife of Pururava, who founded the lunar dynasty to which I belong. You were the mother of Puru from whom I and my brothers descended. So, you are my ancestor.'

Urvashi got up angrily. 'That does not matter. We Apsaras have free will. We are not bound to anyone, nor do relationships define us. I am a damsel, smitten by your handsome appearance, having heard of your valour. I desire you, and there is nothing wrong with it.'

Arjuna again bowed to the lovely timeless beauty and said, 'For me, there is no difference between you and my mother Kunti or mother Gandhari. I consider you a mother and respect you as one. I cannot even dream of looking at you in any other way.'

Urvashi was now furious. She was shaking with anger. Lifting trembling fingers, she pointed them at Arjuna and said, 'You insult me with your words. Even Gods and sages could not resist me, and yet you reject me? Every man would consider it an honour to accept me. You are probably not a man. You don't deserve to be a man. I curse you to become a eunuch since you don't deserve manhood.'

Uttering this curse, Urvashi stormed out of the chambers. A shocked Arjuna walked away from there. He met Chitrasena and reported all that had happened. Chitrasena was perturbed by the turn of events. He took Arjuna to Indra, the Lord of the Celestials.

Indra heard all that had happened and said, 'I asked Chitrasena to send you to Urvashi. I probably made a mistake, and the result is this curse.'

Chitrasena spoke on behalf of Arjuna and told Indra, 'O Indra, please use your powers and render Urvashi's curse invalid. If you fail to do so, the very future of *dharma* on earth is at stake. A strong and brave man is needed to protect *dharma*. If Arjuna becomes a eunuch, it will affect the very future of the earth.'

'I know this, but even I cannot invalidate Urvashi's curse. However, I can modify it using my powers.'

Turning to Arjuna, Indra said, 'Arjuna, you have to be a eunuch, as per Urvashi's curse. But you will not be a eunuch forever. You will have to be a eunuch for one year, and you can choose when you want to give up your manhood. Trust me, this curse will help you in the future.'

Arjuna bowed to Indra, accepting the curse. He had faith in Indra's words. With the weapons he had obtained from the Gods, he was now ready to take on the evil Kauravas when the time came. He knew that Indra would ensure Urvashi's curse would not impede him from achieving his goal.

■

The story of Urvashi's curse is found in the *Aranyaka Parva* of the Mahabharata. This story is not found in the critical edition but is found in most other editions of the epic. This curse turned out to be a major boon for Arjuna, which he found out later. Arjuna invoked this boon when the Pandavas had to spend the thirteenth year of exile in hiding.

He then turned into a eunuch and took the name Brihannala. He joined the royal staff of King Virata as a dance teacher, teaching dance to Virata's daughter. Virata had him examined physically, and when he was satisfied that he was not a man, he was allowed entry into the inner chambers.

During his stay with the Gandharvas, Arjuna learned to sing and dance. He used these skills to the best effect as Brihannala. His expertise in dance led everyone to believe that he was a dance teacher. Since he was in the eunuch form, no one suspected he was Arjuna. The curse thus helped Arjuna spend the thirteenth year of exile without being discovered.

55

How Yama's Boon Helped the Pandavas in Exile

'Stop, stop, catch that deer,' cried a voice.

The Pandava brothers, who were busy repairing the thatched roof of their home, stopped their work to see what happened.

One of the Brahmanas responsible for conducting the fire rituals was shouting, pointing to a deer fleeing towards the forests.

Arjuna ran towards the Brahmana, followed by his brothers, and asked, 'What happened? Why are you so upset?'

'The deer has stolen the *arani* that we use to light the fire to start the homa. How will we start our rituals now? Please retrieve it.'

Hearing these words, Arjuna ran behind the deer. Bheema, Nakula, Sahadeva, and Yudhishtira followed him. From the first day of their exile in the forests, the Pandavas were known for performing many rituals. A large entourage accompanied them to exile including Brahmanas, who conducted daily rituals.

The *arani* was a vital item needed to light the *homa kunda* or fire pit to carry out the fire rituals. They had only one *arani*, which explains why the Pandavas ran behind the deer to bring back the *arani*.

The deer led them on a merry chase and went deep into the forest. Soon, they stopped at a clearing with no sign of the deer. They were exhausted after running such a long distance and upset that they could not find the deer.

The chase left them thirsty, and they needed water, but they could not see any water source nearby. It was a part of the forest they had not been to before.

'Nakula, climb that tree and try to find a lake nearby, so we can quench our thirst,' said Yudhishtira.

Nakula climbed the tree and spotted a lake to the west. He decided to check if the water was drinkable, while his brothers sat below the tree to catch their breath.

When Nakula did not return even after a long time, Yudhishtira was worried and sent Nakula's twin, Sahadeva to find out what had happened.

A long time elapsed, but even Sahadeva did not turn up. Yudhishtira was now seriously worried. He sent Arjuna to check out what happened. When Arjuna did not turn up, Yudhishtira decided to go himself, but Bheema asked him to rest while he went and brought his brothers back.

Even after a long time, Bheema did not return. Yudhishtira was now in a near state of panic. None of his brothers had come back. What could have happened? He decided to check it out himself.

He went in the westerly direction and soon found the lake. What he saw shocked him. All his brothers were lying on the ground. He ran to them and tried to wake them up. He could not sense their breath nor detect a heartbeat. They were all dead!

Who could have killed his mighty brothers? It was unthinkable that anyone could kill the mighty Bheema and the powerful Arjuna. Nakula and Sahadeva were no less brave. Yudhishtira's throat was parched, and he decided to drink some water before finding out what happened.

He heard a voice, as he bent to take water from the lake.

'Stop!'

He looked up and saw a crane on an island in the middle of the lake.

'Who are you, and why do you stop me? What happened to my brothers?'

'This is my lake, and no one can drink water without my permission. I will permit you to drink water only if you can answer my questions. When I told this to your brothers, none of them listened to me, and they arrogantly went ahead and drank the water. The result is before you. What do you choose to do?'

Yudhishtira realised the crane was probably a Yaksha, or a celestial being. He got up and bowed to the crane, 'I am distraught at seeing the bodies of my brothers. But I will not touch this water without answering your questions. Ask whatever you want.'

'What makes the sun rise? What makes the sun set? In whom is the sun established?' asked the crane.

'Brahma makes the sun rise. Dharma makes the sun set, and the sun is established in truth,' replied Yudhishtira.

'What is it that is heavier than the Earth? Which is higher than the Heavens? What is faster than wind? Which is more abundant than grass?'

'Mother is heavier than Earth. Father is higher than the Heavens. Mind is faster than the wind, and our thoughts are more abundant than grass.'

'What is the soul of man? Who is the friend given to a

man by God? What is the main refuge of men?'

'The soul of a man is his son. The wife is a man's friend given by the Gods. Charity is the main refuge of men.'

In this way, the crane asked Yudhishtira many questions, who answered them all and satisfied the crane.

The crane then said, 'Well done! You have successfully answered all my questions. I am happy with your answers. You can drink the water. I also grant you a boon. I can bring back to life any one of your dead brothers. Who do you choose?'

Yudhishtira bowed to the crane and said, 'I choose Nakula.'

'That is surprising. You are in exile. You may have to fight your cousins to get back your empire after the exile. That is when you need Bheema and Arjuna with you. They are born from your mother while Nakula is not, so why did you choose Nakula.'

'O Yaksha, my father Pandu had two wives. I, the son of Kunti, am alive. It is only fair that a son of Madri also survives. That is why I chose Nakula.'

'Well done,' said the crane. 'I am pleased with your answer. You have once again shown why you are the embodiment of *dharma*. I am happy with your conduct, and will restore all your dead brothers to life.'

'Who are you, great one? It is very clear that you are a divine being. Please reveal your identity,' requested Yudhishtira.

The crane disappeared in the blink of an eye, and in its place stood Yamadharma, the God of death and justice. Yama was Yudhishtira's father who had granted Kunti a boon which resulted in Yudhishtira's birth.

Yudhishtira bowed before his celestial father.

'I am pleased with your conduct, my son. Ask for whatever boon you wish.'

'Then I request you to please return the *arani* used to conduct the rituals.'

'It was I who took the *arani* in the guise of a deer,' said Yama with a smile. 'It has been returned to its original place. Ask for another boon.'

'Please help us during the thirteenth year of exile when we need to stay incognito without being recognised.'

'I grant you the boon that you will assume whatever form you want to stay during your year of exile. None will be able to recognise you in the disguise you wear. You will spend the thirteenth year of exile without being detected in the kingdom of King Virata. I grant you this boon. Ask for a third boon.'

'The very opportunity of seeing you is a great boon. Bless me, father, with the ability to conquer greed and anger. May I always be able to practice truth and austerity.'

'You are already endowed with these excellent traits. I grant you your boon.'

With these words, Yama disappeared. Yudhishtira embraced his brothers, who had regained consciousness. Yama's words had filled Yudhishtira with hope that the thirteenth year of exile would pass without problems, allowing them to regain their empire.

■

The incident of the *Yaksha Prashna* is one of the most famous ones in the Mahabharata. It is the last incident of the *Aranyaka Parva* in the Mahabharata. The successful answering of questions by Yudhishtira was one of the three tests by Yama, which he passed.

Yama's boon and his suggestion to go to Matsya kingdom were very helpful. The Pandavas followed this suggestion and spent their thirteenth year of exile in the kingdom of King Virata without being detected.

56

Vyasa Brings Back the Dead

Dhritarashtra lost everything in the 18-day Kurukshetra war between the Pandavas and Kauravas. Every one of his and Gandhari's sons had been killed. His blind love for his son had led to the complete destruction of the Kauravas. Having won the war, Yudhishtira rightfully took over the throne of Hastinapura.

He treated his uncle Dhritarashtra with kindness and respect. After fifteen years in Hastinapura, Dhritarashtra and Gandhari chose to retire to the forest to spend their final days. They were accompanied by Kunti, Vidura, and Sanjaya. The Pandavas were troubled by their mother's departure. Longing to see her and their elders, they went with their families and the widows of the Kauravas to Sage Vyasa's hermitage to meet them.

They spent a long time at the ashrama enjoying the company of their elders. It was time to leave, and everyone assembled to take Vyasa's blessings.

Vyasa told them, 'It has been so many years since the war concluded. Yet you grieve for your lost ones. Emperor Yudhishtira grieves for his son and lost relatives. Dhritarashtra and Gandhari grieve for their lost sons, and Subhadra grieves for her beloved Abhimanyu.'

Everyone nodded their heads. Some women shed tears, remembering their husbands and children who died in the war.

'I have earned a lot of merit by virtue of my austerities. Today, I will use these merits to grant you all a boon. Dhritarashtra, ask for the boon you desire.'

Dhritarashtra bowed to his father Vyasa, and said, 'O, learned sage. I have grieved for a long time at the loss of my son. He was evil, and his actions caused this war. Because of him, so many warriors died in the war. All their loved ones grieve for them. I want to know what happened to them so we can stop grieving for them.'

'I know that all of you are suffering,' said Vyasa. 'I will do something that has never happened before and will never happen again. I will bring back to life all those who were dead. They will wake up as though from a deep sleep. You can spend the night with them. They will leave you forever in the morning.'

The Pandavas and Kaurava family members gratefully bowed to Sage Vyasa for his boon. He instructed them to go to the Ganga, and they followed his guidance.

After bathing in the river and performing evening rituals, they prayed as the sun set. Vyasa entered the river, invoking his divine powers. Suddenly, the waters surged, and from the depths emerged Bheeshma, leading all who had fallen in the war—Drona, Virata, Drupada, Abhimanyu, Ghatotkacha, Duryodhana, Karna, Dushasana, Shakuni, Bhagadatta, and many others who had perished.

Vyasa then used his powers to grant the power of sight to Dhritarashtra and Gandhari. The aged couple saw their beloved Duryodhana, who stood before them, cleansed of his evil and arrogance. They hugged him and wept with joy. They hugged all their sons and other dead relatives.

The Pandavas met Karna, who greeted them with affection. Subhadra and Uttara wept with joy, embracing Abhimanyu. Arjuna saw all his dead sons, including Iravan and Shrutakarma. Draupadi was reunited with her sons, her brothers, and her father.

The long years of mourning lifted as the living and the dead shared one night of peace and reunion. The younger ones took the blessings of the elders. Wives spent joyous moments with their husbands, and children enjoyed the company of their parents and grandparents.

Bheeshma blessed everyone, while Drona was happy to see his favourite Arjuna. After many hours of joyous reunion, it was time to leave. As the sun rose, all those who had come back to life had to return to where they came from.

They went to the world of the Gods, demons, and other celestial beings that was their home.

The wives of many of the Kaurava princes decided to join their husbands. They took the blessings of Vyasa and entered the river, giving up their lives happily, knowing they would be united forever with their loved ones.

As the sage Vaishampayana narrated this tale, there were tears in the eyes of Janmejaya. The story of the remarkable incident where the great Vyasa brought the dead back to life had moved the Emperor.

Janmejaya turned to Vyasa, who was sitting near Vaishampayana. 'O great sage, I am moved by hearing about how you helped my ancestors see their loved ones after their death. I desire to see my father, Parikshith, who was killed by the vile Takshaka. If you grant my boon, I will be blessed.'

Vyasa then obliged Janmejaya and, using his great powers, made Parikshith appear before them. Janmejaya welcomed his father with great joy and took his blessings. He was blessed to see his dear father again and was happy that the snake sacrifice had led to this wondrous occasion.

■

This extraordinary event is recounted in the *Ashramavasika Parva* of the Mahabharata. Vyasa's unmatched powers eased the grief of the Pandavas and Kauravas, offering them a night of miraculous reunion.